Rick Gallop's

Gi DIET

Green-light Cookbook

First published in Great Britain in 2006 by
Virgin Books Ltd
Thames Wharf Studios
Rainville Road
London
W6 9HA

A catalogue record for this book is available from the British Library.

ISBN 0 7535 1180 0
ISBN 9 780753 511800

The paper used in this book is a natural, recyclable product made from wood grown in sustainable forests. The manufacturing process conforms to the regulations of the country of origin.

Designed by Two Associates

Printed and bound in Great Britain by Bath Press

CONTENTS

INTRODUCTION

The Gi Diet is a worldwide bestseller which has sold over 1 1/2 million copies in a dozen languages. Hundreds of thousands of people have been amazingly successful in losing weight on the Gi Diet, and it's not hard to see why.

The plain and simple truth about the Gi Diet is that it works. People find they can lose weight painlessly without going hungry or feeling deprived. And the weight not only comes off, it stays off. This is no fad diet we're talking about, but rather a healthy way of eating that provides the blueprint for an eating lifestyle for your whole life; not just for you, but for the entire family.

As far as mealtimes are concerned, sometimes it's tough going to please everyone all of the time, particularly if you're surrounded by finicky toddlers who turn their nose up at everything, junk food-addicted teenagers who live for chips and hard-to-please partners. But with this programme, nothing could be easier than keeping the whole family happy and healthy.

The other reason the Gi Diet is so successful is that it is extremely simple to follow. This diet is all about the Glycemic Index – the speed at which we digest food and convert it to glucose, the body's energy source. Forget about weighing and measuring food or counting calories, grams or points. All foods have been colour-coded based on how fast or slow they are digested (green, yellow and red) so, as one leading health columnist put it, 'if you can understand a traffic light, you can follow this amazing diet'. Simplicity is a crucial element of this winning formula.

Lastly, unlike many diets, the Gi Diet offers a delicious, nutritious way to approach meals. Why sacrifice flavour and enjoyment in a bid to maintain a svelte silhouette when there is absolutely no need to?

I've received thousands of emails from readers of the *Gi Diet* and a constant thread running through them is a desire for more recipes. We have included some 200 recipes in the three Gi Diet books published to date (*The Gi Diet, Living The Gi Diet* and *The Family Gi Diet*). Now for the first time we are offering a generously illustrated recipe book which features 100 new mouth-watering recipes, such as the quirkily named 'Drunken Salmon', Osso Bucco with Campari or Squash and apple soup. Several recipes are green light versions of popular favourites such as Caesar salad, Chicken tikka or Chocolate pudding, whereas others offer new and exciting taste experiences that will get the whole family rushing to the dining table.

The *Cookbook* is not intended to replace *The Gi Diet*, but to complement it. In *The Gi Diet* you will find far more detailed information than the limited space here can provide, in fact everything you need to know about how the diet works – tips for staying motivated, holidays, celebrations/falling off the wagon, dining out, exercise and frequently asked questions, as well as a comprehensive list of red, yellow and green light foods. If a family focus is important to you, you might want to read the newly released *Family Gi Diet* which includes features on women's health, pregnancy, nursing, menopause, children, from toddlers to teens, spouses/partners and aging issues. Whether overweight or not, every member of the family can benefit from this approach to healthy and nutritious eating.

In this book I have included a brief summary of the essentials of the Gi Diet, along with a guide to shopping and stocking your green light pantry. Those of you who are familiar with the diet can fast forward through this section or stop and leaf through for a little refresher. In addition to the recipes, I've provided a guide to cooking the green light way. So it's all there in black and white for you (or red, yellow and green) – how hard can it be to turn your life around?

One way to get a feel for the Gi Diet and see how it might work for you is to read a few excerpts from some of the emails I have received from readers. These are truly inspirational and have given me a valuable insight into the different ways the Gi Diet is enriching all of your lives. I'm very grateful to you for sharing these stories. If you wish to write to me about your experiences, just go to my website **www.gidiet.com** where you will also find the latest updates on the Gi Diet, readers' comments, professional feedback and the latest developments in health and nutrition. You can also subscribe there to my free quarterly newsletter.

I hope you enjoy these recipes as much as my family does. And again, keep your comments coming – I love to hear from you.

THE GI DIET IN A NUTSHELL

Gi stands for Glycemic Index which is a medical term used to measure the speed at which carbohydrates break down in the digestive system to form glucose (sugar), the body's source of energy – in other words, the fuel that feeds your brain, muscles and other organs. Sugar is set at 100 and all foods are indexed against that number. Therefore, foods that are digested quickly have a high Gi and foods that are digested more slowly have a lower Gi. Below are some popular examples, showing high Gi foods in the left column and low Gi foods in the right.

So what's this got to do with losing weight? Lots, actually! When you eat high Gi foods such as cornflakes, your body rapidly converts it into glucose which dissolves in your bloodstream, spiking your blood sugar level and giving you that familiar sugar rush or high. On the other hand, a low Gi food, such as porridge, will break down more slowly and deliver the glucose into the bloodstream at a slow and steady rate. The chart on page 7 demonstrates the different impact of high and low Gi foods on your blood sugar levels.

The sugar spike, however, is short lived because of a critical enzyme called insulin whose job is to take sugar from the bloodstream and store it for immediate use in your muscles – or as fat around your waist, hips and thighs. The higher the sugar spike, the more insulin is released and the quicker the sugar is drained from your bloodstream, leaving you with a sugar low. And we all know what happens next; you start looking for your next quick sugar fix. This explains why, after your high Gi breakfast of sugary cold cereal, you are reaching for a Danish and coffee as soon as you reach the office. It's simple – a diet of high Gi foods makes you feel hungry more often which means you end up eating more.

Conversely, because they break down more slowly, low Gi foods deliver a steady stream of glucose and do not trigger a sugar spike or flood of insulin. As a result, you feel fuller for a longer period of time, and therefore eat less without going hungry. And eating less without feeling deprived is the key to any successful diet.

Up to now, we have been focusing on carbs (carbohydrates), which account for over half our energy needs. But we also have two other critical food groups to consider, namely proteins and fats.

EXAMPLES OF Gi RATINGS

High Gi		Low Gi*	
Foods	Rating	Foods	Rating
Sugar	100	Orange	44
Baguette	95	All Bran	43
Cornflakes	84	Oatmeal	42
Rice cakes	82	Spaghetti	41
Doughnut	76	Apple	38
Bagel	72	Beans	31
Cereal bar	72	Grapefruit	25
Biscuits (plain)	69	Yoghurt	14

* Any food rating less than 55 in the Gi is considered low

Gi IMPACT ON SUGAR LEVELS

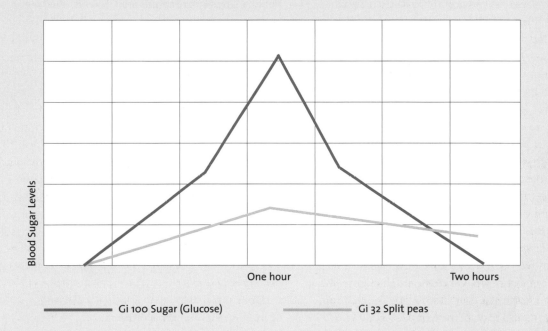

Gi 100 Sugar (Glucose)   Gi 32 Split peas

Proteins are essential for our health. Half of our dry body weight is made up of protein including our muscles, organs, skin and hair. Protein is required to build and repair body tissue. It is also very effective at satisfying hunger as it acts as a brake on the digestive system. So like low Gi carbs, protein helps make us feel fuller for a longer period. Unfortunately, much of our protein comes from animal sources which are usually high in saturated or bad fat. Lean protein found in lean meats, fish, poultry and soya are the best green light choices.

Fat is also essential for our health and body functions. However, many fats are positively dangerous to our health and can significantly increase the risk of heart disease, strokes and some cancers. These fats are called saturated fats and are normally solid at room temperature, for example, cheese, butter and fatty meats. Even worse are trans fats or hydrogenated fats, which have been processed to make them thicken. These are often found in store-bought biscuits, chips and other snacks. Polyunsaturated fats are a far better option, and most vegetable oils fall into this category. Better yet are monosaturated fats, such as olive, rapeseed, peanut, safflower oils, and most nuts – almonds in particular. Omega-3, which is an oil found in deep sea fish such as salmon as well as in flax seed, is great for the health of your heart.

As fats have over twice the calories per gram compared to carbs and proteins, be very careful how much fat you consume.

In short, the ideal combination of foods is low Gi carbohydrates, lean protein, and monosaturated/polyunsaturated fats.

SHOPPING THE GREEN LIGHT WAY

Before you embark on the Gi Diet and start enjoying our delicious recipes, it is important that you have to hand the green light foods you'll need.

The first step, however, is to clear out all those red light foods from your fridge, and give them away to your skinny friends or a food bank or charity (see *The Gi Diet* for a complete list of red, yellow and green light foods). This will not only give you room for your new green light supplies but will also remove temptation. If it's not there, you won't be tempted to eat it! This will also send any family members you share a home with the clear signal that things are about to change for the better.

With the decks cleared, now is the time to go shopping. A word of caution. Do not shop on an empty stomach, otherwise you will run the risk of buying red light ready-to-eat foods. Start as you mean to carry on! Take this book with you to refer to on your first shopping trip, along with your shopping list. Choosing green light foods will soon become second nature. Many people have found the compact and inexpensive *Gi Diet Shopping and Eating Out Pocket Guide* helpful.

So, you're standing at the entrance of the supermarket wondering what to do next. Luckily, we've organised your buying trip in the next few pages, by following the traditional aisle layout of most stores. We've listed your best green light choices on pages 14 – 17.

Because there are literally thousands of different brands, we haven't attempted to list them. Instead, we have grouped all foods under their categories; e.g. Cold Cereals rather than Kellogg's Cornflakes; Crispbreads rather than Ryvita. Occasionally we will list a brand for clarification when it is an outstanding best buy.

Sometimes it can be a little tricky to distinguish green light choices within a category or between competing brands. Bread is a classic example. Bread made from white flour is low in fibre and is red light. Wholegrain bread, on the other hand, which is high in fibre, is green light. The difficulty is that some apparently healthy 'seven grain' breads are not what they seem.

Some of them list 'enriched white flour' or 'unbleached flour' as the principal ingredient, which make them red light. The first ingredient listed on bread should always be '100% wholemeal flour' or '100% wholegrain flour'. If 'stoneground' is mentioned, even better.

READING LABELS

It's important to check the list of ingredients on labels. Here are some simple guidelines to follow:

SERVING SIZE
Is the serving size realistic, or is the manufacture lowering it (as is often the case with cereals) so that the calorie and fat totals, in particular, appear more favourable to a Gi Diet than the competition? When comparing one brand with another, make sure you are comparing the same serving sizes.

CALORIES (KCALS)
The product with the least amount of calories is obviously the best choice.

FAT
Choose the product with the least amount of fat, particularly saturated (bad) fat. Avoid any product that contains trans fats – the worst of all the saturated fats.

PROTEIN
The higher the protein level, the better. Protein acts as a brake on the digestive system and lowers the Gi rating.

FIBRE
The product with the higher fibre content is the best choice, whether it's soluble or insoluble. Fibre, like protein, significantly lowers the Gi rating.

SUGAR

Try to avoid products that contain added sugar. Choose the ones with sugar substitutes or none at all. 'Non-fat' products that contain added sugar can still be fattening.

SODIUM (SALT)

Look for lower sodium levels. Sodium increases water retention, which causes bloating and adds weight – not very helpful when you're trying to lose it – and has an adverse effect on blood pressure. If you are at risk for heart disease, stroke or high blood pressure, this is a particularly important issue for you.

NUTRITIONAL INFORMATION

TYPICAL VALUES PER PACKET

Energy	1237kj / 298kcal
Protein	8.9g
Carbohydrate	17.5g (of which sugars 4.2g)
Fat	21.3g (of which saturates 4.4g)
Fibre	1.6g
Sodium	0.1g

TYPICAL VALUES PER 100g

Energy	2474kj / 595kcal
Protein	17.8g
Carbohydrate	35.0g (of which sugars 8.4g)
Fat	42.6g (of which saturates 8.8g)
Fibre	3.2g
Sodium	0.2g

The Food Standards Authority has provided some useful additional guidelines on what constitutes 'a lot' (high quantities) or 'a little' (low quantities) of the following nutrients

FOOD STANDARDS AUTHORITY GUIDE

BASED ON 100G SERVINGS

	High	Low
Fat	20g	3g
Saturated Fat	5g	1g
Sugars	10g	2g
Salt	1.25g	0.25g

FRUIT/VEGETABLE AISLE

Fruit and veg represent the cornerstone of the Gi Diet. Unfortunately, most of us limit our choices to a narrow selection. Break with tradition and explore the wonderful selection of vegetables and fruits from literally around the world.

They are low Gi and high in fibre, nutrients, vitamin C and minerals. Cooking them raises their Gi and reduces their nutrient content, so use as little water as possible and cook only until they are just tender – or try eating them raw.

Soya-based foods such as tofu are high in protein, low in saturated fat and are good for a healthy heart. When selecting the tofu, choose the soft version rather than the firm as it has a lower fat level. Many supermarkets carry something known as Textured Vegetable Protein (TVP) which is used to make veggie burgers and breakfast sausages, among other things. It's an excellent choice whether you're vegetarian or not. Quorn is also a popular alternative.

You can often find nuts and dried fruit in the produce or home-baking section of the supermarket. Most dried fruit is very high in sugar and therefore red light. However, there are some good yellow light choices and all dried fruit can be used in modest quantities in baking.

Nuts are an excellent source of good fats and proteins. Green light nuts contain even more monosaturated (best) fat than the other nuts. Remember, though, that all nuts are calorie dense and must be eaten in limited quantities, about a modest handful per serving. It's just too easy to consume a whole bowl of nuts while watching television without even being aware of it; this quantity would equal your total calorie needs for an entire day!

THE DELI COUNTER

Most processed meats are high in fat, sodium and sodium nitrate and are therefore red light. There are, however, a few green light options. Cheese is a dietary villain, since it's high in saturated fat and calories. For flavour it can be used sparingly, sprinkled on salads, omelettes and pasta.

THE BAKERY

Anything that is made up primarily of bleached white flour – which has one of the highest Gi ratings of any food – is red light. Because most people are in the habit of eating white bread, which has been stripped of most of its nutrients, they're not used to the taste of wholegrain breads. Once you've tried it, you'll soon discover that a wholegrain loaf (green light) is far more flavoursome than a bland white loaf (red light).

Always check labels when choosing a loaf. The first ingredient should always be 100% wholemeal or wholegrain flour, and there should be a minimum of 2.5 to 3.0g of fibre per slice.

While all the desserts you'll find in the bakery

section are red light because of the white flour and sugar in them, you can still make delectable desserts at home, using the delicious recipes on pages 144–155.

THE FISH COUNTER

All fish and shellfish are green light and offer a great variety of choice for wonderful meals. Do not bread or batter fish. You will find tasty fish and seafood recipes on pages 112 –123.

Some people are under the mistaken belief that oily fish such as salmon and mackerel aren't good for you. In fact, oily fish is rich in omega-3 and is therefore extremely beneficial for heart health.

THE MEAT COUNTER

Meat always contains some fat, but certain cuts have far less fat than others. By simply trimming visible fat, you can reduce the overall amount by an average of 50%. Remember to keep the serving size down to 120g (4oz), which is about the size of the palm of your hand.

Skinless chicken or turkey breast is really the benchmark for low-fat protein. Dark meat, (chicken or turkey thighs and legs, duck and goose), is higher in saturated fat and therefore not a good option.

TINNED BEANS & VEGETABLES AISLE

Beans, or legumes, are the perfect green light food. They are rich in protein and fibre, and low in fat. While dried beans are your best choice, using well rinsed and drained tinned beans is perfectly acceptable. Likewise, with vegetables, it is always preferable to buy them fresh or frozen rather than tinned. Tinned tomatoes are the one exception to this rule.

PASTA & SAUCES AISLE

Most pasta is green light, in particular wholemeal pasta. Make sure you always undercook it slightly – pasta should be *al dente*, as the Italians say, or firm to the bite. Watch the serving size; 40g (1 1/2oz) uncooked per serving.

Seasoning mixes with no
added sugar
Spices

BAKING SUPPLIES
Almonds
Baking powder
Cashews
Cocoa
Hazelnuts
Macadamia muts
Oat bran
Pumpkin seeds
Sunflower seeds
Wheat bran
Wheat germ
Wholemeal flour

CEREALS & BREAKFAST FOODS AISLE
CEREAL
100% bran
All-Bran
Bran buds
Fibre 1

Fibre First
Large flake oatmeal
Oat bran
Steel-cut Irish oatmeal

SPREADS & JAMS
Fruit spreads/Jams (extra
fruit, no added sugar)

BEVERAGES AISLE
BEVERAGES
Bottled water (sparkling
or still)
Decaffeinated coffee
Diet soft drinks (without
caffeine)
Herbal teas
Iced tea (with no
added sugar)
Light instant chocolate
Tea (with or without
caffeine)

DAIRY CABINET
MILK
Buttermilk
Skimmed milk
Soya milk (plain, low-fat)

CHEESE
Cheese (fat-free)
Cottage cheese (1% or
fat free)

Extra low-fat cheese (e.g.
Laughing Cow light,
Boursin Light)
Low-fat soya cheese

YOGHURT & SOUR CREAM
Fruit yoghurt (non-fat with
sugar substitute)
Sour cream (non-fat)

BUTTER & MARGARINE
Soft margarine
(non-hydrogenated light)

EGGS
Egg whites
Liquid eggs

FROZEN FOOD SECTION
VEGETABLES
Asparagus
Beans (green/runner)
Broccoli
Brussels sprouts
Carrots
Cauliflower

Okra
Peas
Peppers
Spinach

PREPARED FOODS
Chicken souvlaki
Extra-lean burgers
Frozen fish without
breaded coating
Quorn
Scallops and prawns
without breaded coating
Veggie burgers
Textured Vegetable Protein

DESSERTS
Frozen soya desserts with
less than 100 calories
per 120g (4oz)
Ice cream (low-fat and no
added sugar) e.g. Wall's
Soft Scoop

FRUIT
Black berries
Blueberries
Cherries
Cranberries
Peaches
Raspberries
Rhubarb
Strawberries

INTRODUCTION TO GREEN LIGHT COOKING

The notion of going on a diet can be a daunting one. People are often fearful that their food choices will be limited to unappetising, bland, and difficult to prepare meals. Not so with the Gi Diet! Just look at what's listed in the green light shopping list and you will see that there really is a wide ranging variety of delicious foods. You can eat extremely well on the Gi Diet and never have to sacrifice flavour or convenience. Not only are green light foods high in fibre, low in saturated fat, and low in sugar, but they are also some of the best tasting foods around. Extra virgin olive oil, for example, is a monosaturated (or "best") fat which adds a wonderful robust flavour to many dishes.

I have been fortunate enough to have found a talented cook, Laura Buckley, to help develop the recipes in this book. She has worked with both my wife, Ruth, and myself to build upon our personal favourite meals as well as the thousands of suggestions we have received from readers.

The key guidelines in developing these recipes, other than being green light, were all based on taste. Fresh herbs, exciting spices and ethnic flavours all play a major part in this collection of recipes. Not that we've ignored old favourites such as Coffee-spice-rubbed chicken breasts or Orange and cranberry bran muffins which have been given a new spin.

You can also adapt your own favourite recipes by using less fat – especially saturated fats like butter or lard – avoiding white flour and sugar, while adding extra fibre.

Although the emphasis here is on cooking from scratch, this doesn't mean you'll be tied to the kitchen. Most of the recipes can be made in under 30 minutes, many even less. Breakfast recipes such as Breakfast in a glass or Gi Granola can be put together on the hop while others such as Oaty buttermilk pancakes and Berry-stuffed French toast are for those weekend mornings when time is not at such a premium.

There are lots of soup and salad choices for lunch and a whole range of dinner choices including fish and seafood, meat, poultry and meatless meals.

Desserts are actively encouraged on the Gi Diet, so we have given you a generous range of delicious choices including Apple upsidedown cake or Oatmeal chocolate chunk cookies. Also as snacks are an essential part of the programme – 3 per day – you will find some surprises here, too. How about Smoked salmon and dill scones or Cranberry-almond biscotti?

My family have had a field day trying out all the recipes. I'll let you find your own favourites but I have to admit the Drunken Salmon was a real hit on the barbecue – credit for the title goes to Ruth!

Here are some tips on ingredients, equipment and side dishes. You'll also find helpful advice on food preparation and cooking throughout the recipes.

INGREDIENTS

You will notice that not all of the ingredients in the recipes are strictly green light. Occasionally I have added wine, even whisky, for depth of flavour as well as small amounts of sauces that contain sugar and dried fruit. This doesn't mean that the recipe is yellow or red light. The quantities are small enough that they'll have little or no effect on your blood sugar levels, keeping these recipes firmly green light. To replace sugar in recipes, I've had great success cooking with Splenda, a derivative of sugar but without the calories, and have found its flavour excellent. Look for the granular type because it is the easiest to use. Measure all the major sugar substitutes in *equal volume to sugar, not in equal weight to sugar*; i.e. 1 tablespoon of sugar equals 1 tablespoon of sweetener. To keep things simple, we've used level tablespoons (15ml) for all those measurements using sugar substitutes.

EQUIPMENT

NON-STICK FRYING PANS

When cooking low-fat dishes, non-stick frying pans are key. You need only use a minimal amount of oil when cooking with them. Using an oil spray (or sometimes none at all), food slides right off the pan. The recommended cooking heat for non-stick surfaces is no higher than medium. For high, use only non-abrasive utensils and brushes. Wash your pan with hot soapy water and a nylon brush and do not put it in the dishwasher as this will damage its non-stick coating.

GRILL PANS AND INDOOR GRILLS

The same rules for caring for your non-stick pans apply to grill pans and indoor grills. When using them, you need only apply a light brush or spray of oil. A grill pan allows the fat from the food you are cooking to drain away from the food.

SIDE DISHES

Almost all the dinner recipes I have included in this book should be accompanied by side dishes, particularly salads.

PORTIONS

Remember – a quarter of your plate should be filled with carbohydrates such as pasta, rice or boiled new potatoes. Since overcooking tends to raise the Gi level of food, boil pasta until it is just *al dente*, or firm to the bite, and take rice off the heat before it starts to clump together.

A quarter should contain lean protein – 120g (4 ounces), or what would fit in the palm of your hand.

The remaining half your plate should be filled with green light vegetables and salads. Again, don't overcook the veggies; they should be tender crisp. Most people will choose vegetables cooked this way over mushy, flavourless vegetables any day.

VEGETABLE PREPARATION

You can cook vegetables in any of the following ways:
- **To boil vegetables:** in a saucepan of boiling water, cook the vegetables for 5–7 minutes or until they are just tender.

| ■ Meat | ■ Vegetables | ■ Potato / pasta / rice |

- **To steam in a saucepan:** boil 3cm (1in) of water. Place a steamer basket filled with the vegetables in the saucepan. Cover and steam for five to seven minutes or until the vegetables are just tender.
- **To microwave vegetables:** place the vegetables in a large plate or bowl. Add 60mls (2fl.oz) of water. Cover with clingfilm and microwave (on high) for about 3–5 minutes or until the vegetables are just tender. To dress them up and add some zing, drizzle them with lemon juice and add pepper. Add a lettuce leaf to frozen peas when you cook them and they will come out tasting as fresh.

RECIPE SERVINGS

While many of the recipes are for 4 servings, we have indicated where recipes can be divided and/or frozen.

THE GOLDEN RULES OF DINING

Here are 5 golden mealtime rules which will help you get the most benefit from the Gi Diet.

1

DRINK A GLASS OF WATER
Always drink a glass of water (240ml/ 8oz) with your lunch and dinner. Drink early on in the meal as this will fill your tummy and help you feel fuller, sooner.

2

DIVIDE YOUR PLATE IN THREE
Imagine your plate divided into three section: half a plateful containing vegetables (at least two); one-quarter protein (meat, fish, poultry, soy); one-quarter potato, rice, pasta.

3

WATCH YOUR SERVING SIZES
VEGETABLES: as much as you'd like.
MEAT/FISH/POULTRY: 120g (4 ounces) or the size of the palm of your hand or a pack of cards.
RICE: 50g (1 3/4oz) uncooked
PASTA: 40g (1 1/2oz) uncooked
POTATOES: 2 to 3 small

4

DON'T RUSH YOUR MEALS
It takes up to half an hour for the stomach to tell the brain that it's full. Most of us eat more than we need before the 'stop eating' message gets through. So eat slowly, or at least put the fork/spoon down between mouthfuls. Meals are not pit stops. Slow down and savour your food.

5

EAT 3 MEALS AND 3 SNACKS A DAY
Always eat three meals and three snacks daily. Breakfast is critical as you probably haven't eaten for 10 hours or so and if you miss it, you will be starving and risk pigging out on the wrong foods later in the day. Slow and steady stays the course.

If you follow the five golden rules with your green light menu, then you will lose weight painlessly without going hungry or feeling deprived. Literally thousands of readers have written to me saying that they can't believe they are actually on a diet, eating all this food and never going hungry. They also swear they will never return to their old eating habits! Losing weight and keeping it off has never been so easy. This is the way you will eat for the rest of your life.

Now for the recipes. Let me know your favourites – check the website **www.gidiet.com** for details on how to get in touch with me. Enjoy!

BREAKFAST AND BRUNCH

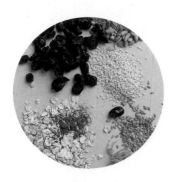

Gi GRANOLA

There are so many uses for this granola beyond serving it for breakfast with skimmed milk or low-fat yogurt. Sprinkle it on fruit salad or low-fat, no-sugar ice cream, or eat a couple of handfuls as a snack.

200g (7oz) jumbo porridge oats
1x40g pack dried apple rings, chopped or 75g (3oz)
   dried cranberries or raisins
60g (2½oz) sunflower seeds (unsalted)
50g (2oz) sesame seeds
60g (2½oz) chopped almonds
50g (2oz) ground flaxseeds or linseeds
1tbsp ground cinnamon
2tsp grated orange zest
½tsp sea salt
1 large egg white
1tbsp vegetable oil
1tbsp clear honey
2tsp frozen orange juice concentrate
1tsp vanilla essence

1 Preheat the oven to 190°C, Gas 5. In a large bowl, mix together the oats, apple, sunflower seeds, sesame seeds, almonds, flaxseeds or linseeds, cinnamon, orange zest and salt.
2 In a small bowl, whisk together the egg white, oil, honey, orange juice concentrate and vanilla essence. Pour into the oat mixture and toss until thoroughly coated. Turn out onto a shallow baking tray lined with nonstick parchment and spread evenly. Bake for 25–30 minutes, turning the mixture once with a spatula halfway through baking time, or until mixture is golden brown.

Storage: Store in an airtight container for 2 days at room temperature or freeze for up to 1 month.

Makes about 475g (serves about 12)

OATY BUTTERMILK PANCAKES

This delicious pancake recipe was inspired by a recipe sent in by a reader, Jo-Ann. It's another way to get your oats, and a great weekend brunch treat. Serve with fruit yogurt and fresh fruit.

75g (2¹/₂oz) jumbo porridge oats
500ml (18fl.oz) buttermilk*
160g (5¹/₂oz) wholemeal flour
40g (1¹/₂oz) ground linseed or flax powder
1tbsp sugar substitute
1tsp cinnamon
1tsp bicarbonate of soda
1tsp baking powder
¹/₄tsp sea salt
2 large eggs
2tbsp vegetable oil
1tsp vanilla essence

1 In a bowl, soak the oats in buttermilk for 20 minutes.
2 In a large bowl, mix together the flour, linseed, sugar substitute, cinnamon, bicarbonate, baking powder and salt. In another bowl, whisk together the eggs, oil and vanilla essence. Stir the soaked oats and buttermilk. Pour this mixture over the flour mixture and stir until just mixed to a batter.
3 Heat a nonstick griddle or large frying pan over a medium heat. Ladle about 4tbsp of the batter onto the griddle or pan for each pancake. Cook until bubbles appear on top, about 2 minutes.
4 Using a spatula, flip the pancakes and cook for another 2 minutes, or until golden. Transfer to a plate and cover with a tea towel to keep warm. Repeat with remaining batter.

*if buttermilk is not available use 250ml skimmed milk plus 1tbsp (15ml) lemon juice or white vinegar. Let stand for 10 minutes.

Makes about 16 pancakes (4–6 servings)

TOFU BREAKFAST BURRITO

The filling of this is also good on its own as a vegetarian version of scrambled eggs.

1 tbsp olive oil
1 small onion, chopped
½ a red pepper, chopped
1 clove garlic, finely chopped
2 x 250g packs pressed tofu, crumbled
½ tsp ground turmeric
2 drops hot pepper sauce, or to taste
Pinch each of sea salt and freshly ground black pepper
50g (2oz) low-fat Cheddar cheese
3 soft wheat tortillas, or 3 wholemeal pittas, halved
Salsa to serve

1 In a nonstick frying pan, heat the oil over a medium-high heat. Cook the onion, red pepper and garlic for 8 minutes or until softened. Mix in the tofu, turmeric, hot pepper sauce and seasoning. Cook for 5 minutes or until heated through and any liquid is evaporated. Check for seasoning.
2 Divide the filling among the tortillas, sprinkle with cheese and roll up, or stuff into pittas. Serve with salsa.

Serves 6

HERBED CHEESE OMELETTE

To make this even lower fat, you can use all egg whites. You can substitute peeled prawns for the chicken breast, or add in some chopped red pepper and/or celery with the spinach.

2 egg whites
1 egg
1 tbsp chopped fresh basil (optional)
1 tsp grated lemon zest
1 tsp lemon juice
2 tbsp herb-flavoured low-fat soft cheese (e.g. light Boursin)
Pinch of sea salt and freshly ground black pepper
1 tsp olive oil
About 50g (2oz) spinach leaves, chopped
25g (1oz) cooked chicken breast or ham, chopped

1 In a bowl, combine the egg whites, egg, 1tbsp water, basil (if using), lemon zest, juice, cheese and seasoning. Using a fork, stir just until blended and the cheese is broken up into smaller lumps.
2 In a small nonstick omelette or frying pan, heat the oil over a medium-high heat. Add the spinach, then cover and cook for about 2 minutes or until the spinach is wilted. Pour in the egg mixture and cook, uncovered, for about 5 minutes, lifting the edges to allow the uncooked eggs to run underneath, until almost set.
3 Add the chicken over half of the omelette. Using a spatula, fold over the other half and cook for 1 minute. Slide onto a warmed plate.

Serves 1

FRUITY PORRIDGE

A satisfying hot breakfast for when there's a chill in the air. You can substitute apples, peaches or nectarines for the pears. You can substitute other dried fruits or a mixture of a few different kinds.

150g (5oz) jumbo porridge oats
500ml (18 fl oz) skimmed milk
2 Comice or Conference pears,
   cored and chopped
1 x 75g pack dried cranberries
1tsp ground cinnamon
 tsp ground nutmeg
Sugar substitute, to taste
   (optional)

1 Place oats on rimmed baking sheet and toast in oven at 140°C, Gas 1 for 20 minutes. (Oats can be toasted ahead and stored in an airtight container for up to 1 week.)
2 In large saucepan, bring milk and 500ml (18 fl oz) water to boil. Stir in oats, pears, cranberries, cinnamon and nutmeg and return to boil. Reduce heat to low and cook, stirring occasionally, for 20 minutes or until thickened and oats are tender. Stir in sugar substitute to taste, if desired.

Storage: Can be made ahead and chill for up to 1 day. Reheat, adding a little more milk or water to thin to desired consistency.

Serves 4

BREAKFAST IN A GLASS

This is a great make-and-take breakfast for mornings on the run. It packs protein, fruit and fibre in one glass. Look for whey or soy protein isolate* in your local health food store.

450ml (16fl.oz) soya milk
500g (18oz) fresh or frozen
   mixture 'fruits of the forest'
   berries (raspberries,
   blueberries, blackcurrants,
   strawberries, etc.)
1/2 a banana
125g (4oz) low-fat natural yogurt
25g (1oz) flaxseeds or linseeds
2tbsp sunflower seeds
25g (1oz) whey or soy protein
   isolate powder*
2tbsp soy lecithin granules
   (optional)
Sugar substitute to taste

1 Using a blender or liquidiser, whiz together the soya milk, berries, banana and yogurt until almost smooth.
2 In a spice or coffee grinder, finely grind the flaxseeds or linseeds and sunflower seeds. Add to the soya milk mixture in the blender along with the protein powder and lecithin, if using. Blend just until mixed, about 5 seconds.

*As an alternative you can use silken tofu

Serves 2

BAKED EGGS IN HAM CUPS

This dish is perfect for brunch entertaining served on a bed of dressed mixed greens.

6 large slices lean Black Forest or Parma ham, unbroken if possible
3 large eggs
4 egg whites
3tbsp skimmed milk
3 spring onions, chopped
1tbsp grated Parmesan cheese
¼ tsp each sea salt and freshly ground black pepper

1 Heat the oven to 200°C, Gas 6. Carefully press 1 slice of ham into 6 lightly greased muffin cups or deep bun tins, ensuring the ham sticks up over the edges.
2 In a bowl, whisk together the eggs, egg whites and milk. Stir in the onions, Parmesan and seasoning.
3 Pour the egg mixture evenly among the ham cups. Bake for 15 minutes or until a knife inserted in the centre comes out clean. Carefully remove from the pan using 2 spoons.

Serves 6

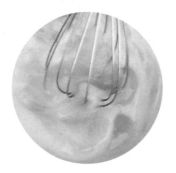

CRUSTLESS QUICHE

This easy quiche is great warm or cold. It also pairs well with a side salad for lunch or a light supper.

1tsp soft margarine
25g (1oz) fresh wholemeal
    breadcrumbs
1 head of broccoli, trimmed and
    cut into florets
3 eggs and 3 egg whites
250ml (9fl.oz) skimmed milk
¼tsp fine sea salt
¼tsp freshly ground
    black pepper
2 slices fresh wholemeal
    bread, cubed
6 sun-dried tomatoes, soaked in
hot water, drained and chopped
2 spring onions, chopped
50g (2oz) feta cheese, crumbled

1. Grease the bottom and sides of a deep 25cm (10-inch) pie plate with margarine. Add the breadcrumbs and shake to coat the bottom and sides evenly. Preheat the oven to 190°C, Gas 5.
2. Steam the broccoli for 5 minutes or until just tender. Rinse under cold water, drain and chop. Set aside.
3. In a large bowl, whisk together the eggs, egg whites, milk and seasoning. Stir in the cubed bread, sun-dried tomatoes, onions and feta. Pour into the prepared pie plate.
4. Bake for 50–60 minutes or until light golden, puffed and just set in the centre.

Smoked salmon variation: Omit the broccoli, sun-dried tomatoes and feta. Stir in 125g (4oz) chopped smoked salmon and 2tbsp chopped fresh dill into the egg mixture.

Serves 6

BACON AND EGG MUFFINS

1tsp olive oil
1 onion, chopped
1 fresh green chilli, seeded and
    finely chopped (optional)
4 rashers unsmoked back
    bacon, chopped
1x350g jar artichoke hearts,
    drained and chopped
50g (2oz) reduced-fat Cheddar
    cheese
40g (1½oz) wheat bran
40g (1½oz) chopped fresh
    basil or parsley
4 eggs
4 egg whites
180ml (6fl.oz) skimmed milk
1tsp freshly ground black pepper

1. Line a 12-hole muffin or deep bun tin with 12 paper baking cases. Preheat the oven to 180°C, Gas 4.
2. In a nonstick frying pan, heat the oil over a medium-high heat. Cook the onion, chilli (if using) and bacon for 5 minutes or until softened. Transfer to a bowl and allow to cool for 5 minutes. Stir in the artichokes, cheese, wheat bran and basil.
3. In a separate bowl, whisk together the eggs, egg whites, milk and pepper. Pour onto the bacon and onion mixture and stir until well combined. Ladle or spoon into the muffin cups, filling to the top.
4. Bake for 25 minutes or until the filling is firm and the tops are lightly browned. Let cool on a rack for 5 minutes. Remove the muffins from the tin and allow to cool completely.

Storage: Wrap the muffins individually in plastic wrap and refrigerate for up to 2 days, or freeze for up to 1 month.

Makes 12 muffins

BERRY-STUFFED FRENCH TOAST

This is a perfect dish for brunch entertaining. Keep the finished toasts piled up on a baking sheet in a warm oven until ready to serve.

For the berry filling:

500g (1lb 2oz) mixed red or 'fruits of the forest'-style berries (fresh or frozen)
3tbsp sugar substitute
1tsp grated lemon zest
1tbsp cornflour

For the French toast:

3 eggs
4 egg whites
500ml (18fl.oz) skimmed milk
1tbsp sugar substitute
2tsp vanilla extract
1tsp ground cinnamon
About 2tbsp vegetable oil
12 slices wholemeal bread

1 To make the berry filling: In a saucepan over a medium heat, combine the berries, sugar substitute and lemon zest; cook for about 5 minutes or until the berries have released some of their juice.

2 In a small bowl, blend the cornflour with 1tbsp of juice from the berries; stir into the berry mixture. Increase the heat to high and cook, stirring constantly, for about 5 minutes or until thickened. Remove from the heat and set aside to cool.

3 To make the French toast: In a large bowl, whisk together the eggs, egg whites, milk, sugar substitute, vanilla and cinnamon.

4 Brush 1tsp oil onto a nonstick griddle or a large nonstick frying pan over a medium-high heat. Dip the bread one slice at a time into the egg mixture, pressing down and letting soak for 10 seconds, then turn and press again for 10 seconds. Lift out, letting the excess mixture drip back into the bowl.

5 Fry the soaked bread slices, 2–4 slices at a time depending on the pan size, for about 3 minutes until lightly browned. Spread a slice with about 2tbsp filling and top with another slice, browned-side up, like a sandwich, pressing down lightly to firm. Continue frying for 3 minutes, then turn the sandwich over and fry for 3 minutes longer or until golden brown on both sides. Repeat with the remaining bread slices, brushing the griddle with more oil as needed.

6 Put any leftover berry filling in a bowl to serve alongside the toasts.

Serves 6

SOUPS

CREAMY SEAFOOD CHOWDER

I love chowders on a winter's day – one of the great comfort foods. Don't be alarmed at the long ingredient list. This is an easy soup to make and everyone will love it.

2tbsp olive oil
1 onion, chopped
1 clove of garlic, finely chopped
2 sticks of celery, chopped
1 large carrot, chopped
40g (1½oz) wholemeal flour
750ml (1¼pints) fish or chicken stock
250g (9oz) baby new potatoes, scrubbed
2tsp freshly chopped oregano (or ½tsp dried)
½tsp salt, ½tsp pepper
4 bay leaves
250g (9oz) haddock fillet or other firm white fish, cut in chunks
250g (9oz) shelled prawns or scallops (or mixture of both)
250ml (9fl.oz) skimmed milk
180g (6oz) fresh or frozen and thawed sweet corn
2tbsp grated fresh Parmesan
3tbsp chopped fresh parsley
4–6tbsp half-fat crème fraîche, optional

1 In a heavy saucepan, heat the oil over a medium heat; cook the onion and garlic until softened, about 3 minutes. Add the celery and carrot; cook for 2 minutes. Stir in the flour and cook, stirring, for 1 minute. Add the stock, potatoes, oregano, bay leaves, salt and pepper and bring to the boil; reduce the heat and simmer, covered, for 15 minutes or just until the potatoes are tender.
2 Add the fish and shellfish; cook for 3 minutes or until opaque. Stir in the milk and corn, and heat through. Stir in the Parmesan and parsley. Serve with a dollop of crème fraîche if using.

Serves 6 – 8

LEMONY LENTIL AND RICE SOUP

1tbsp olive oil
1 onion, chopped
1 clove of garlic, finely chopped
1 large carrot, chopped
1tsp curry powder (or to taste)
2 litres (3 pints) chicken stock
200g (7oz) Puy or green lentils,
    rinsed
85g (3oz) brown basmati rice
1 bay leaf
1tbsp chopped fresh thyme
4tbsp fresh lemon juice
Sea salt and freshly ground
    black pepper

1 In a large heavy saucepan, heat the oil over a medium heat; cook the onion and garlic until softened, about 3 minutes. Add the carrot and curry powder, and cook for 2 minutes.
2 Add the stock, lentils, rice, bay leaf and thyme; simmer, covered, for 40–45 minutes or until the lentils and rice are tender. Remove the bay leaf. Add the lemon juice and season to taste with salt and pepper.

Serves 8

QUICK AND EASY CHICKEN NOODLE SOUP

Who doesn't love chicken soup? On a miserable winter's day nothing tastes better and this version is easy. Enjoy.

2tsp olive oil
2 carrots, chopped
2 sticks of celery, chopped
3 cloves of garlic, chopped
1 onion, chopped
1tbsp chopped fresh thyme
1.5 litres (2 3/4 pints)
    chicken stock
350g (12oz) skinless, boneless
    chicken breast, diced
200g (7oz) frozen peas
60g (2 3/4 oz) small pasta shapes
4tbsp chopped fresh parsley
Sea salt and freshly
    ground pepper

1 In a large saucepan, heat the oil over a medium-high heat. Add the carrots, celery, garlic, onion and thyme, and cook for 10 minutes or until the vegetables are slightly softened.
2 Pour in the stock and bring to the boil. Reduce the heat to simmer and add the chicken, peas and pasta. Simmer for 15 minutes until chicken is just firm and the pasta is *al dente*. Stir in the parsley, check for seasoning and serve.

Serves 6

MISO AND SEA VEGETABLE SOUP

Sea vegetables, such as kombu and arame (or dulse), are a great source of calcium and other nutrients. They can be found in Asian food stores and some larger supermarkets. If they are not available in your area, just follow the variation below.

10g (1/3 oz) arame or dulse
3 pieces kombu, about 15cm
   (6 inches) long
2tsp vegetable oil
1 leek (white and light-green part
   only), finely chopped
2 carrots, thinly sliced

1/2 a red pepper, cored
   and chopped
100g (3 1/2 oz) fresh shiitake
   mushrooms, thinly sliced
2tsp grated fresh root ginger
2 spring onions, chopped
75g (2 3/4 oz) miso paste

1 Cover the arame or dulse with 250ml (9fl.oz) cold water for 10 minutes then drain.
2 In a large soup pot, combine 1.5 litres (2 1/2 pints) water and kombu. Bring to boil, then reduce the heat and simmer for 20 minutes. Remove the kombu and discard.
3 Meanwhile, in a nonstick frying pan, heat the oil over a medium heat. Cook the leek, carrots, red pepper, mushrooms and ginger for 5 minutes or until softened. Stir in the arame. Add the vegetables to your kombu broth.

4 In a small bowl, whisk together the miso and about 250ml (9fl.oz) broth taken from the soup pot, then stir back into the soup. Add the onions and simmer very gently for 1 minute (do not allow to boil – it will destroy the flavour and beneficial enzymes in miso).

Variation if kombu, arame and miso paste are not available: **Replace the water and kombu broth with hot chicken or vegetable stock. Replace the arame with 300g (10oz) baby spinach, finely chopped. Add to the broth when adding the vegetables. Simmer for 5 minutes or until the spinach is tender.**

Serves 6

ORANGE-SCENTED BROCCOLI AND LEEK SOUP

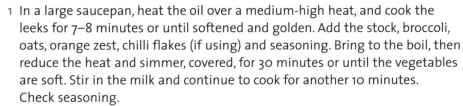

2tbsp olive oil
4 medium leeks, trimmed and thinly sliced
1.5 litres (2½ pints) chicken stock
400g (14oz) broccoli florets, chopped small
100g (3½ oz) jumbo porridge oats
Zest of 1 medium orange
½tsp hot chilli flakes, or to taste
½tsp sea salt
½tsp ground black pepper
500ml (18fl.oz) skimmed milk
50g (2oz) reduced-fat Cheddar cheese (optional)

1 In a large saucepan, heat the oil over a medium-high heat, and cook the leeks for 7–8 minutes or until softened and golden. Add the stock, broccoli, oats, orange zest, chilli flakes (if using) and seasoning. Bring to the boil, then reduce the heat and simmer, covered, for 30 minutes or until the vegetables are soft. Stir in the milk and continue to cook for another 10 minutes. Check seasoning.
2 Serve each bowlful with a sprinkle of cheese, if liked, and extra freshly ground pepper.

Serves 6 – 8

MUSHROOM SOUP WITH ROASTED GARLIC AND GINGER

This soup tastes even better the next day when the flavours have had time to infuse. For a heartier dish, add chopped cooked chicken, cooked prawns or cubed tofu.

10g (¹/₃oz) dried porcini/ceps mushrooms
10g (¹/₃oz) dried shiitake mushrooms
1 head of garlic
1tbsp vegetable oil
250g (9oz) fresh shiitake mushrooms, sliced
1.7 litres (3 pints) chicken or vegetable stock
2tbsp grated fresh ginger
1tbsp soy sauce
2tbsp rice wine vinegar
2tsp mirin or dry sherry
¹/₄tsp freshly ground black pepper
3 spring onions, sliced thinly

1 In a bowl, soak the dried mushrooms in 250ml (9fl.oz) of boiling water for 30 minutes. When cool, remove the mushrooms and slice or chop. Reserve with the liquid.
2 Heat the oven to 190°C, Gas 5. Wrap the garlic in foil and bake for 30 minutes or until the cloves are completely soft. Squeeze the softened garlic from the cloves into a small bowl and set aside.
3 In a soup pot, heat the oil over medium-high heat. Add the fresh shiitake mushrooms and cook for 5 minutes or until softened. Add the stock, dried mushrooms and soaking liquid, ginger, roasted garlic, soy sauce, vinegar, mirin and pepper; stir. Bring to the boil, reduce the heat and cook, covered, for 20 minutes. Stir in the sliced onions.

Serves 4

SPINACH AND MEATBALLS SOUP

For the meatballs:

250g (9oz) lean minced beef
25g (1oz) fresh wholemeal breadcrumbs, from
    half a slice of bread
2tbsp chopped fresh parsley
1 large egg
1 small onion, grated
1 clove garlic, finely chopped
1tsp ground cumin
1tsp sea salt
½tsp freshly ground black pepper

For the soup:

2tbsp olive oil
1 onion, chopped
1 clove garlic, finely chopped
2tbsp tomato purée
300g (10oz) baby leaf spinach
3tbsp chopped fresh parsley
2tbsp chopped fresh coriander
1x400g can cannellini beans, drained and rinsed
¼tsp ground cumin
1.5 litres (2¾ pints) chicken or beef stock
3tbsp lemon juice
¼tsp each sea salt and freshly ground
    black pepper
125g (4oz) strained yogurt, optional
    (see recipe p.157)

1 In a large bowl, whisk the egg with a fork. Add
the breadcrumbs, parsley, onion, garlic, cumin
and seasoning; stir to combine. Add the meat
and mix well with clean hands. Shape
teaspoonfuls of mixture into balls and set aside.

2 In a large saucepan, heat the oil over a medium-
high heat. Add the onion and garlic and cook for
4–5 minutes or until softened. Stir in the
tomato purée, cumin, spinach, parsley and
coriander and continue cooking for another 2
minutes until the spinach is wilted. Add the
stock and seasoning.

3 Drop in the meatballs and beans, and bring to
the boil. Reduce the heat, cover and simmer for
20 minutes or until the meatballs are firm and
no longer pink inside. Stir in the lemon juice.
Check seasoning and serve with a dollop of
strained yogurt, if liked.

Serves 6

SQUASH AND APPLE SOUP

1 tbsp olive oil
1 x 2.5kg (2 1/2 lb) butternut
   squash, peeled and seeded
2 medium leeks, trimmed
1 onion, chopped
1 medium carrot
1 tbsp grated fresh ginger
1 tbsp chopped fresh thyme
1/2 tsp dried sage
1 large apple, peeled and cored
1 litre (1 3/4 pints) chicken or
   vegetable stock
250ml (9fl.oz) apple juice
1 x 400g can cannellini beans
Chopped fresh chives
Sea salt and freshly ground
   black pepper

1 Chop the leeks (white and light-green parts only) and cut the butternut squash, carrot and apple into 1cm (1/2-inch) cubes.
2 In a large saucepan, heat the oil over a medium-high heat. Add the squash, leeks, onion, carrot, ginger, thyme and sage; cook for 10 minutes or until the vegetables are slightly softened. Stir in the apple.
3 Pour in the stock and apple juice and bring to the boil. Reduce the heat, cover and simmer, stirring occasionally, for 20 minutes or until the vegetables are tender.
4 Pour half of the soup into a blender or food processor and purée until smooth. Return the purée to the saucepan, add the beans and cook for 2 minutes over a medium heat until hot and bubbling. Check seasoning and serve sprinkled with the chopped chives.

Serves 8

VEGETABLE BARLEY SOUP AU PISTOU

1 tbsp olive oil
1 medium leek (white and light-
green part only), chopped
2 carrots, chopped
2 sticks celery, chopped
1/2 a red pepper, chopped
1 medium courgette, chopped
2 sprigs fresh thyme
1.5 litres (2 3/4 pints)
   chicken stock
125g (4oz) green beans, fresh
   or frozen
100g (3 1/2 oz) pearl barley
2 tbsp tomato purée
1/2 tsp sea salt, 1/4 tsp freshly
ground black pepper
4 tbsp Gi Pesto (see page157)

1 In a large heavy saucepan or soup pot, heat the oil over a medium heat; cook the leek, carrots, celery, red pepper, courgette and thyme for about 8 minutes or until softened.
2 Add the stock, green beans, barley, tomato purée and seasoning to taste, then bring to the boil. Reduce the heat, cover and simmer for 45 minutes or until the barley is tender. Remove the thyme stalks and stir in the pesto.

Serves 6

SALADS
AND SIDES

SUMMER MEDITERRANEAN SALAD

This recipe comes from our daughter-in-law Jennifer – a fabulous cook!
This salad is most delicious at the height of the summer. You can easily
make substitutions too. If you don't have yellow or orange peppers,
substitute green or red peppers, while red onion could easily replace the
sweet onion.

3 medium tomatoes, cut into chunks
1 cucumber, cut into 2cm (1-inch) chunks
1 yellow pepper, cored and cut into 2cm (1-inch) chunks
1 orange pepper, cored and cut into 2cm (1-inch) chunks
½ a sweet onion (such as Vidalia), thinly sliced
85g (3oz) pitted black olives
4tbsp fresh basil, cut into thin strips
4tbsp chopped fresh parsley
4tbsp extra-virgin olive oil
3tbsp balsamic vinegar
¼tsp freshly ground black pepper
¼tsp sea salt
125g (4oz) feta cheese, preferably reduced fat, crumbled

1 In a large bowl, mix together the tomatoes, cucumber, peppers, onion,
   olives, 3tbsp basil and the parsley. Add the olive oil, vinegar, salt and pepper,
   and toss gently. Taste and adjust seasoning.
2 Just before serving, sprinkle with feta and the remaining basil.

If you prefer a more marinated salad, you can complete step 1 of this recipe
several hours in advance.

Serves 4

CELERIAC SLAW

This salad makes a nice change from the usual cabbage coleslaw. Look for celeriac that is firm and heavy for its size and one with few roots and knobs to make peeling easier. Work as quickly as possible because peeled celeriac tends to discolour.

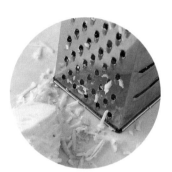

1 celeriac, about 500g, peeled and grated
1 large apple, grated (unpeeled)
2 sticks celery, chopped
1 green or red pepper, cored and chopped
2 spring onions, chopped
4tbsp chopped fresh parsley
25g (1oz) sunflower seeds
For the dressing:
4tbsp extra-virgin olive oil
3tbsp reduced-fat mayonnaise
2tbsp white wine vinegar
1tbsp whole grain mustard
1tbsp lemon juice
½tsp sea salt
½tsp freshly ground black pepper

1 For the dressing, stir together the olive oil, mayonnaise, vinegar, mustard, lemon juice and seasoning to taste.
2 Put the celeriac, apple, celery, green or red pepper, spring onions, parsley and sunflower seeds into a large bowl. Mix in the dressing and serve.

Storage: Can be covered and refrigerated for up to 1 day.

Serves 6

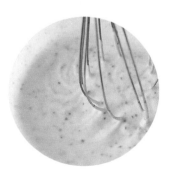

WHEAT BERRY SALAD WITH ROASTED RED PEPPER DRESSING

125g (4oz) wheat grains or
  wheat berries
1/2 a red pepper, grilled
  and skinned
1 clove garlic, finely chopped
2tbsp balsamic vinegar
1tbsp fresh orange juice
4tbsp extra-virgin olive oil
1/4 tsp sea salt
A pinch of freshly ground
  black pepper
1 red onion, chopped
1 tomato, chopped
1 avocado, chopped
2tbsp chopped fresh coriander

1 In a saucepan, bring the wheat grains to a boil with 1 litre (1 3/4 pints)
   of lightly salted water. Reduce the heat to low and cook, covered,
   for 1 hour or until tender. Drain and place in a bowl.
2 Meanwhile, put the roasted red pepper, garlic, balsamic vinegar,
   orange juice, olive oil, and salt and pepper in a food processor; purée
   until smooth. Pour over the wheat grains and toss to coat. Add the red
   onion, tomato, avocado and coriander; stir to combine.

This can be covered and chilled for up to 1 day.

Serves 4–6

RAITA SALAD

Based on the refreshing Indian condiment, this salad pairs well with the Coffee-Spice-Rubbed Chicken Breasts on page 71.

300g (10oz) baby spinach
1/2 a cucumber, quartered
lengthwise and sliced into 1cm
(1/4 -inch) chunks
2 tomatoes, chopped
1/2 a red onion, thinly sliced
1x200g pot low-fat yogurt
1/2 tsp ground cumin
1/4 tsp sea salt

1 In a large bowl, toss together the spinach, cucumber, tomatoes and
   red onion.
2 In another bowl, stir together the yogurt, cumin and salt. Add to the
   spinach mixture and toss to coat.

Serves 4

LEMONY STIR-FRIED VEGETABLES

You can substitute any green-light vegetable you like.

2tbsp olive oil
2 carrots
1 red, yellow, green or
    orange pepper
1 medium courgette, halved
    lengthwise
10 fresh shiitake mushrooms,
    stems trimmed and sliced
1tbsp grated fresh ginger
1 clove of garlic, finely chopped
150g (5oz) mangetouts, trimmed
4 spring onions
Juice and grated zest of one lemon
1tbsp soy sauce
3tbsp sesame seeds, toasted

1 Prepare the vegetables: slice the carrots, courgette and spring onions on the diagonal, and core and slice the pepper.
2 In a wok or large nonstick frying pan, heat the oil over a medium-high heat. Add the carrots, peppers, courgettes, mushrooms, ginger and garlic. Stir-fry for 2–3 minutes.
2 Add the mangetouts and spring onions, then stir-fry for another 2–3 minutes or until the vegetables are just softened.
4 Stir in the lemon zest, juice and soy sauce. Cook for 1 minute.
5 Sprinkle in the sesame seeds, tossing to coat the vegetables. Serve immediately.

Serves 4–6

ROASTED FENNEL AND ORANGE SALAD

This falls somewhere between a salad and a side dish, and is great as a starter for a dinner. It pairs well with grilled fish.

2 medium bulbs of fennel
2 oranges
75g (3oz) pitted black olives
250ml (9fl.oz) dry white wine
    or vermouth
3tbsp olive oil
3 cloves of garlic, finely chopped
1tbsp grated orange zest
1tsp fresh thyme leaves
1/2tsp each sea salt and
    freshly ground black pepper

1 Preheat the oven to 190°C, Gas 5. Snip the feathery tops from the fennel and reserve for garnish. Trim the base of the fennel. Cut each bulb into quarters and then each quarter into eighths. In a pot of boiling, salted water, cook the fennel for 5 minutes; drain and place in a baking dish or roasting pan large enough to hold the fennel in one layer.
2 Cut a slice from the top and bottom of each orange and discard. Cut away the peel from the oranges so no white pith remains, then slice into 5mm (1/4-inch) thick rounds. Add to the baking dish along with the olives.
3 In a small bowl, whisk together the wine, olive oil, garlic, orange zest, thyme, salt and pepper. Pour evenly over the fennel mixture. Cook in the top third of the oven for 30–40 minutes or until the fennel is tender and golden at the edges. Garnish with the reserved fennel tops and serve hot or at room temperature.

Serves 4–6

RED BEAN TABBOULEH

This is a light, yet satisfying salad that could also could be served as a main course. You could use it as the stuffing in a wholewheat tortilla or in lettuce wraps.

150g (5oz) bulgur wheat
1tsp sea salt
1x400g can red kidney beans, drained and rinsed
4 plum tomatoes, chopped
3 spring onions, chopped
40g (1½oz) bunch fresh parsley, destalked and roughly chopped
25g (1oz) bunch fresh basil, destalked and chopped
4tbsp extra-virgin olive oil
2tbsp lemon juice
¼tsp freshly ground black pepper
Lettuce leaves and lemon wedges for garnish

1 In a large bowl, combine the bulgur and salt. Stir in 500ml (18fl.oz) boiling water and stand for 15–20 minutes or until the liquid is absorbed and bulgur is tender. Fork through the grains to separate.
2 Mix in the beans, tomatoes, onions and herbs. Drizzle over the olive oil and lemon juice, sprinkle with the pepper and stir to combine. Taste and adjust seasoning if necessary.
3 Line the plates or a platter with lettuce leaves and pour the bean salad over the top. Garnish with lemon wedges.

This will keep well in the refrigerator for up to 2 days.

For variation, you could add a cucumber, chopped into bite-sized pieces, or replace the parsley with chopped fresh coriander or mint.

Serves 6

ROASTED GREEN BEAN, TOMATO AND SHIITAKE FRICASSEE

This side dish is delicious and goes well with a simple grilled chicken breast.

500g (1lb 2oz) whole green beans, trimmed
2 medium tomatoes, cut into eighths
2tsp plus 3tbsp olive oil
1 red onion, chopped
2 cloves of garlic, finely chopped
250g (9oz) fresh shiitake mushrooms, sliced
1tbsp fresh lemon juice
120ml (4fl.oz) dry white wine or vermouth
1tbsp chopped fresh basil
Sea salt and freshly ground pepper

1 Preheat the oven to 200°C, Gas 6. Arrange the green beans and tomatoes on a baking sheet. Drizzle with 2tsp olive oil and toss to coat. Season and roast for 10–12 minutes or just until tender.
2 Meanwhile, in a frying pan, heat the remaining oil over a medium-high heat. Add the onion and garlic, and cook for 1 minute. Add the mushrooms and cook until softened, about 5–7 minutes.
3 Add the lemon juice, then pour in the wine and cook until wine is absorbed, about 2–3 minutes. Add the green beans, tomatoes and basil; toss. Season to taste and serve.

Makes 4 servings

MIXED GREENS WITH ROASTED PEARS, PECANS AND CHÈVRE

3 ripe but firm Comice
  or Conference pears
2tsp olive oil
About 250g (9oz) mixed salad
  leaves, washed and dried
40g (1 1/2oz) goats' cheese
50g (2oz) pecan halves,
  lightly toasted
For the dressing:
2tbsp apple juice
1tbsp balsamic vinegar
1/2tsp honey or sugar substitute
Pinch each sea salt and
  ground black pepper
3tbsp extra-virgin olive oil

1 Preheat the oven to 220°C, Gas 7. Quarter and core the pears then cut each quarter in half lengthwise. Place on a baking sheet and bake for 15–20 minutes or until the pears are tender and turning golden brown. Set aside to cool.
2 To make the dressing: In a small bowl, whisk together the apple juice, vinegar, honey (or sugar substitute) and seasoning, then whisk in the olive oil.
3 When ready to serve, toss the salad greens with the dressing and divide among your plates. Arrange the pear slices over the top and sprinkle with crumbled goats' cheese and pecans.

Serves 6

CAESAR SALAD

3 slices wholemeal bread
2tsp olive oil
Pinch each of sea salt and
  freshly ground black pepper
1 large head of romaine or
  cos lettuce
For the dressing:
3 cloves of garlic, finely chopped
3 anchovy fillets, finely chopped
2tbsp tahini
1tsp Dijon mustard
1/2tsp Worcestershire sauce
1/2tsp each sea salt and freshly
ground black pepper
3tbsp lemon juice
1–1 1/2tbsp extra-virgin olive oil

1 Heat the oven to 180°C, Gas 4. Cut the bread into 1cm (1/2-inch) pieces and place in a bowl. Add the olive oil, salt and pepper and toss to coat well. Arrange in a single layer on a rimmed baking sheet.
2 Bake for 20 minutes or until golden and crisp, then cool.
3 Tear the lettuce into bite-sized pieces and place in a large bowl.
4 To make the dressing: In a bowl, stir together the garlic, anchovies, tahini, mustard, Worcestershire sauce, salt and pepper. Whisk in the lemon juice, 2tbsp warm water and the olive oil.
5 Pour the dressing over the lettuce and toss to coat. Sprinkle with your croutons before serving.

Serves 4

CURRIED QUINOA SALAD

160g (5¼oz) quinoa,
　rinsed and drained
100ml (3½fl.oz) olive oil
1 large shallot or medium
　onion, chopped
1tsp mild or medium
　curry powder
2tbsp lemon juice
1tsp Dijon mustard
¼tsp sea salt

¼tsp freshly ground
　black pepper
1 small carrot, finely chopped
½ a red pepper, finely chopped
50g (1¾oz) dried apricots, chopped
50g (1¾oz) unsalted cashews,
　toasted and chopped
2tbsp chopped spring onion
1tbsp chopped fresh parsley

1　In a deep-sided frying pan over a medium heat, 'roast' the quinoa for 5 minutes or until fragrant and beginning to pop. In a small saucepan, bring 500ml (18fl.oz) of water and a pinch of salt to the boil. Add the roasted quinoa; cover and simmer over a medium heat for 15–20 minutes or until the water has been absorbed. Scrape the quinoa into a large bowl and let it cool.

2　Meanwhile, in a nonstick frying pan, heat 1tbsp oil over a medium-high heat; cook the shallot for 3 minutes or until softened. Stir in the curry powder and cook, stirring, for another 2 minutes. Remove from the heat and set aside.

3　In a small bowl, whisk together the remaining olive oil, lemon juice, mustard, salt and pepper and pour it over the quinoa. Fork through the carrot, red pepper, apricots, cashews, spring onion and parsley.

Storage: This can be covered and chilled for up to 3 days.

Serves 6

POULTRY

CHICKEN TIKKA

This recipe uses garam masala, an Indian spice mixture with myriad uses. You can buy it, but the home-made version on page 157 is far superior.

125g (4oz) strained yogurt (see recipe page 157)
2 cloves garlic, finely chopped
1tbsp grated fresh ginger
2tsp lemon juice
1tsp sea salt
½tsp ground cumin
½tsp chilli powder
½tsp garam masala (store-bought or see recipe, page 157)
¼tsp ground turmeric
500g (1lb 2oz) boneless, skinless chicken breasts, cut in bite-sized cubes

1 In a bowl, stir together the yogurt, garlic, ginger, lemon juice, salt, cumin, chilli powder, garam masala and turmeric. Add the chicken and toss to coat thoroughly with the mixture. Cover and chill for 4–6 hours.
2 Remove the chicken from the marinade and thread onto 4 metal kebab sticks or wooden skewers soaked in cold water.
3 Heat the oven to 200°C, Gas 6. Place the kebabs on a nonstick baking sheet and bake for 10–12 minutes or until the chicken is firm and no longer pink inside. (You can also grill them over a medium-high heat.)

Vegetarian option: **Substitute pressed smoked tofu for chicken.**

Serves 4

SPICY ROASTED CHICKEN WITH TOMATOES AND TARRAGON

Dinner at our friend Meryle's is always a culinary treat, and this is one of her recipes. Serve this dish with basmati rice or quinoa to soak up the sauce.

250g pack cherry tomatoes, halved
4tbsp olive oil
5 cloves of garlic, finely chopped
2tbsp chopped fresh tarragon
1-2tsp hot red chilli flakes, or to taste
1tsp each sea salt and freshly ground black pepper
4 boneless, skinless chicken breasts, about 125g (4oz) each

1 Heat the oven to 230°C, Gas 8. In a large bowl, toss the tomatoes with the olive oil, garlic, 1tbsp tarragon and chilli flakes.
2 Place the chicken on a rimmed baking sheet. Pour the tomato mixture over the chicken, arranging the tomatoes in a single layer around the meat. Sprinkle with salt and pepper.
3 Roast for 30–35 minutes or until the chicken is no longer pink inside. Transfer the chicken to a platter. Spoon over the tomatoes and roasting juices, sprinkle with the remaining tarragon and serve.

Serves 4

FRUIT-AND-NUT STUFFED TURKEY BREAST

This is a great Gi alternative to the traditional holiday bird. Serve it with vegetables and Cranberry and Orange Sauce (page 157).

1 boneless skinless turkey breast,
   about 1kg (2¼lb)
2tsp olive oil
250ml (9fl.oz) chicken stock
125ml (4fl.oz) dry cider or apple juice
1tbsp cornflour
Sea salt and freshly ground black pepper

For the stuffing:
1tbsp olive oil
1 onion, chopped

1 clove of garlic, chopped
1 thick slice of wholemeal bread, crusts removed
   and cubed
25g (1oz) dried apple rings, chopped
50g (2oz) dried cranberries
50g (2oz) unsalted shelled pistachios,
   roughly chopped
2tsp chopped fresh thyme
1tsp dried sage
¼tsp ground black pepper
4tbsp chicken stock

1 To make the stuffing: In a nonstick frying pan heat the oil over a medium-high heat and cook the onion and garlic for 5 minutes until softened. Stir in the bread, apples, cranberries, pistachios, thyme, sage, pepper and chicken stock, stirring until absorbed. Set aside and cool.

2 Using a chef's knife, cut along the edge of one side of the turkey breast. Continue to slice in half almost all the way through. Open the meat like a book and hit the flesh with a meat mallet or rolling pin to flatten slightly.

3 Spread the stuffing mixture evenly over one half of the breast. Fold the other half over the stuffing and, using kitchen string, tie the breast at evenly spaced intervals to fully enclose the stuffing in the breast. Rub with olive oil and season lightly.

4 Heat the oven to 170°C, Gas 3. Place the turkey on a rack set in a small roasting pan and roast for 45 minutes. Remove the pan from the oven and pour in 250ml stock. Roast for another 30 minutes or until a meat thermometer inserted in the centre of the roast reaches 80°C. Remove to a wooden board; cover loosely with foil and stand for 15 minutes.

5 Meanwhile, place the roasting pan over a medium heat. Stir the cider or apple juice into the pan juices and bring to the boil, scraping up any brown bits from the bottom of the pan. In a small bowl, whisk together the cornflour and 1tbsp water. Whisk this paste into the pan juices and bring to the boil, stirring for 1 minute or until thickened slightly and glossy. Boil for 1–2 minutes until lightly thickened.

6 Slice the turkey into 1cm (½-inch) thick slices and serve with the sauce spooned over.

Serves 6–8

CHICKEN AND SPINACH ROTOLO

A novel way to use lasagne sheets. Serve with a green salad and enjoy.

12 wholemeal lasagne sheets
400g (14oz) leaf spinach
2tbsp olive oil
1 onion, chopped
2 cloves garlic, finely chopped
250g (9oz) mushrooms, thinly sliced
1 green pepper, cored and chopped
500g (1lb 2oz)skinless, boneless chicken breasts,
    diced small
2x400g cans chopped tomatoes
½tsp dried oregano
½tsp dried basil

4tbsp reduced-fat cream cheese
6tbsp skimmed milk
1tbsp grated Parmesan cheese
50g (2oz) reduced-fat mozzarella cheese,
    grated or chopped
1tbsp chopped fresh parsley

For the tomato sauce:
1tbsp olive oil
Pinch of sugar substitute
1tbsp chopped fresh basil
Sea salt and pepper to taste

1   In a large pot of boiling salted water, cook the lasagne sheets according to pack instructions until *al dente*. Drain and rinse under cold water. Lay flat on damp tea towels and set aside.
2   Meanwhile, blanch the spinach in a pan of boiling water until wilted then drain, squeeze dry and chop.
3   In a large nonstick frying pan, heat the oil over a medium-high heat. Cook the onion, garlic, mushrooms and green peppers for about 8 minutes or until lightly browned. Add the chicken and cook for 5 minutes until golden brown. Stir in the spinach, a third of the tomatoes, the milk, cream cheese, oregano, basil, salt and pepper; cook until any liquid has evaporated, about 8–10 minutes. Remove from the heat and stir in the Parmesan.

4   To make the tomato sauce: In a nonstick frying pan, heat the oil over a medium-high heat. Add the remaining tomatoes, sugar substitute, basil and seasoning. Simmer, stirring occasionally, for 15minutes or until thickened. Spread evenly in the bottom of a 23x33cm (9x13-inch) ovenproof baking dish.
5   Divide the chicken mixture evenly along each lasagne sheet. Then roll up from the short end and stand upright on the sauce in the baking dish. Sprinkle with mozzarella, cover and cook in the oven at 190°C, Gas 5 for 15 minutes. Uncover and continue cooking for 5 more minutes or until the cheese is melted and golden brown. Sprinkle with parsley to serve.

Serves 6

COFFEE-SPICE-RUBBED CHICKEN BREASTS

You can make a large batch of the rub, minus the coffee, and keep in an airtight container for up to 3 months.

1tbsp olive oil plus extra to grease
4 skinless, boneless chicken breasts, about 125g (4oz) each
1tbsp freshly ground coffee
1tsp paprika
1tsp ground cumin
½tsp chilli powder
½tsp ground coriander
¼tsp cinnamon
⅛tsp ground cloves
¼tsp sea salt
¼tsp freshly ground black pepper
2 cloves garlic, finely chopped

1 Preheat the grill to a medium-high heat and lightly brush the rack with a little oil.
2 Place the chicken breasts between 2 sheets of nonstick baking paper or clingfilm and, using a meat mallet or rolling pin, beat until about 1cm (½ inch) thick.
3 In a small bowl, mix together the coffee, paprika, cumin, chilli powder, coriander, cinnamon, cloves, salt, pepper and garlic. Stir in 1tbsp olive oil to make a smooth paste. Rub the mixture evenly into both sides of the chicken breasts.
4 Cook the chicken under the heated grill until no longer pink inside, about 3–4 minutes per side.

Make-ahead tip: After coating with the rub, the chicken can be wrapped and refrigerated for up to 4 hours before cooking.

Serves 4

CHICKEN STIR-FRY WITH BROCCOLI

1 egg white
1tsp Chinese spice mix (page 83, optional)
500g (1lb 2oz) skinless, boneless chicken breast,
    cut into bite-sized pieces
3tbsp orange juice
2tbsp soy sauce
1tbsp Hoisin sauce
1tbsp oyster sauce
2tsp cornflour
1tsp sesame oil

1tbsp vegetable oil
1 onion, thinly sliced
2 cloves of garlic, finely chopped
1tbsp grated fresh ginger
1 red pepper, cored and sliced
1 head of broccoli, stalks trimmed and cut
    into small florets
75g (3oz) fresh bean sprouts
50g (2oz) coarsely chopped cashews

1 In a medium bowl, whisk together the egg
  white and spice mix, if using. Add the chicken
  and toss to coat well. Set aside.
2 In a small bowl, stir together the orange juice,
  soy sauce, Hoisin sauce, oyster sauce, cornflour
  and sesame oil until smooth. Set aside.
3 In a wok or large nonstick frying pan, heat the
  oil over a high heat. Add the chicken and stir-fry
  for 5 minutes until just firm. Set aside.Add the
  onion, garlic, ginger, and red pepper to the pan
  and stir-fry for 1 minute. Add the broccoli and
  4tbsp water and bring to the boil. Cover and
  cook for 5 minutes or until the broccoli is just
  tender and the water is evaporated.

4 Return the chicken and sauce. Stir-fry for 3
  minutes or until the sauce is thickened and the
  chicken is cooked through. Mix in the bean
  sprouts and cashews, then serve.

Serves 4

SPINACH-STUFFED CHICKEN BREASTS

Oats are an unlikely ingredient in a savoury sauce, but work well here as
a thickener and give an extra hit of fibre.

2tbsp olive oil
2 onions, chopped
1 clove garlic, finely chopped
125g (4oz) leaf spinach, chopped
1tbsp chopped fresh mint leaves
¼tsp *herbes de Provence*
½tsp sea salt
½tsp freshly ground black pepper
4 skinless, boneless chicken breasts
   125g (4oz) each

50g (2oz) light Boursin cheese
1tbsp grated fresh Parmesan
1 red pepper, cored, quartered and roasted
120ml (4fl.oz) white wine
120 ml (4fl.oz) chicken stock
2x400g cans chopped tomatoes
¼tsp crumbled saffron strands
50g (2oz) large-flake oats

1 Heat 1tbsp oil in a large nonstick frying pan over
   a medium-high heat. Cook half of the onion and
   all of the garlic until softened, about 5 minutes.
   Add the spinach and cook, stirring, until wilted,
   about 2 minutes. Stir in the mint, *herbes de
   Provence*, and ¼tsp each of salt and pepper.
   Transfer to a bowl and set aside to cool.
2 Meanwhile, place the chicken between 2 sheets
   of nonstick baking paper or clingfilm and, using
   a rolling pin or mallet, beat the flesh until quite
   thin, about 5mm (¼inch) thick.
3 Add both cheeses to the spinach mixture and
   stir to combine. Divide the mixture evenly
   among the chicken breasts and spread almost
   to the edges. Cut the pepper in strips and lay on
   top. Starting from the short edge, roll up the
   chicken breasts and seal, placing join-side down
   on a cutting board. Sprinkle with the remaining
   salt and pepper.

4 Heat the remaining olive oil in a large nonstick
   frying pan over a medium-high heat. Cook the
   remaining onion until softened, about 5
   minutes. Add the wine, chicken stock, tomatoes,
   saffron and a little more seasoning. Simmer,
   covered, for 8 minutes, then stir in the oats.
5 Arrange the chicken rolls on top of the sauce
   and continue to simmer, covered, for 20–25
   minutes or until the chicken is cooked through.
   To serve, place the chicken on a plate and spoon
   sauce around and over the top.

Serves 4

73

TURKEY-QUINOA LOAF

Quinoa improves the nutritional profile of this meatloaf.
Leftovers are great cold.

85g (3oz) quinoa, rinsed and drained
250g (9oz) turkey mince
1 apple, peeled and grated
1 onion, finely chopped
3 spring onions, chopped
1 clove garlic, finely chopped
2tbsp finely chopped fresh sage
1tsp Worcestershire sauce
1tsp sea salt
1/2 tsp freshly ground black pepper
1/4 tsp ground allspice
1/4 tsp ground cloves

1 In a frying pan over a medium heat, toast the quinoa for 5 minutes or until
   fragrant and beginning to pop. In a small saucepan, bring 250ml (9fl.oz)
   water and a pinch of salt to the boil. Add the toasted quinoa, then cover
   and simmer over a medium heat for 15–20 minutes or until the water
   has been absorbed. Set aside.
2 Preheat the oven to 180° C, Gas 4. In a large bowl, mix together the turkey,
   apple, onion, spring onion, garlic, sage, Worcestershire sauce, seasoning and
   spices. Add the quinoa and mix in thoroughly.
3 Pack the mixture into a nonstick 1kg (2lb) loaf tin. Bake for 1 hour or until
   a meat thermometer registers 70°C when inserted in the centre of the
   meatloaf. Serve with Cranberry and Orange Sauce (see recipe on page 157).

Muffin Loaf Option: Place the mixture into 12 deep bun tins or muffin cups
and bake for about 30 minutes or until a meat thermometer registers 70°C
when inserted in the centre of the muffin.

Serves 6

CHICKEN SCHNITZEL WITH ORANGE AND APRICOT SAUCE

4 boneless skinless chicken breasts
60g (2 1/2 oz) wholemeal flour
1/2 tsp each sea salt and freshly
ground black pepper
2 egg whites
25g (1oz) wheat bran
25g (1oz) wheat germ

3tbsp fine dry wholemeal breadcrumbs
1tsp grated orange zest
1tbsp olive oil
120ml (4fl.oz) fresh orange juice
120ml (4fl.oz) chicken stock
100g (3 1/2 oz) dried apricots, thinly sliced
3 spring onions, chopped

1 Using a meat mallet or rolling pin, pound the chicken breasts between 2 sheets of clingfilm or nonstick baking paper until it is the thickness of a £1 coin.

2 In a large shallow dish, combine the flour and seasoning. In another shallow dish, whisk the egg whites. In a third dish, combine the wheat bran, wheat germ, breadcrumbs and orange zest.

3 Pat the chicken dry and dredge in the flour, shaking off any excess. Dip in the eggs, letting the excess drip off, then dredge in the wheat-bran mixture, coating completely.

4 In a large nonstick frying pan, heat the oil over a medium-high heat. Fry the chicken (in batches if necessary) for 4 minutes per side or until golden brown and just cooked through. Transfer the schnitzel to a platter and place in a low oven to keep warm.

5 In the same pan, add the orange juice, chicken stock and apricots. Bring to the boil and reduce until slightly thickened and syrupy, about 3 minutes. Stir in the onion. Serve the schnitzel with the sauce poured over the top.

Serves 4

CHICKEN AND SWISS CHARD LASAGNE

There can never be too many ways to make lasagne. We vary the vegetables depending on what we have in the pantry but this combination is always a hit. You can also use minced turkey instead of chicken.

1tbsp plus 2tsp olive oil
4 large onions, thinly sliced
1tsp sugar substitute
1tsp balsamic vinegar
3/4tsp freshly ground black pepper
500g (1lb 2oz) minced chicken
120ml (4fl.oz) red wine
250g (9oz) mushrooms, sliced
1 clove garlic, finely chopped
1 bunch Swiss chard, chopped, or 1x225g bag leaf
   spinach, chopped
2x400g cans chopped tomatoes
1tbsp each chopped fresh rosemary and oregano,

   or 1tsp each dried
1/2tsp sea salt
1x250g tub low-fat cottage cheese
12 wholemeal lasagne sheets

For the béchamel sauce:
6tbsp vegetable oil
85g (3oz) wholemeal flour
1 litre (1 3/4 pints) skimmed milk, warmed
2tbsp grated fresh Parmesan
1/4tsp sea salt
1/4tsp freshly ground black pepper
Pinch of nutmeg

1 Heat 1tbsp oil in a nonstick frying pan over a medium-high heat. Cook the onion for 10 minutes or until softened and turning golden brown. Sprinkle with the sugar substitute, then reduce heat to low and cook, stirring occasionally, for 15 minutes or until a deep amber colour. Stir in the balsamic vinegar and 1/4tsp pepper. Remove from heat and set aside.

2 Heat 2tsp oil in another large nonstick frying pan over a medium heat; cook the chicken until browned, stirring to break it up, about 8–10 minutes. Add the red wine, mushrooms, garlic and Swiss chard or spinach; cook, stirring occasionally, until the mushrooms are softened, about 8 minutes. Add the tomatoes, rosemary and oregano, salt and remaining pepper; bring to the boil. Reduce the heat and simmer, covered, for 25 minutes. Remove from the heat and stir in the cottage cheese.

3 To make the béchamel sauce: Heat the oil in a saucepan on a medium-high heat. Add the flour and cook, stirring, for 1 minute. Slowly pour in

the milk and cook, whisking gently, until the mixture is thickened and smooth. Add the Parmesan, salt, pepper and nutmeg. Remove from the heat.

4 Meanwhile, in a large pot of boiling water, cook the lasagne sheets for about 10 minutes or until *al dente*. Drain and rinse under cold water. Lay the sheets flat on damp tea towels and set aside.

5 Preheat the oven to 190°C, Gas 5. Ladle some of the meat sauce into the bottom of a 23x32cm (9x13-inch) ovenproof glass baking dish. Lay 3 sheets side by side on top of the sauce. Spread with more meat sauce, then a quarter of the béchamel sauce and half of the onions. Repeat with pasta sheets, meat sauce, béchamel sauce and onions ending with béchamel sauce. Cover the dish with foil and place on a roasting pan to catch any drips. Bake for 45 minutes, then uncover and bake for 15 minutes, or until golden brown on top. Cool for 10 minutes before serving.

Serves 8

MEAT

ROASTED PORK TENDERLOIN
WITH BALSAMIC GLAZE AND GINGERED PEACH SALSA

We love serving this dish when the peaches are at their summer best, but it is great any time. Serve with basmati rice, fresh asparagus and a side salad.

120ml (4fl.oz) balsamic vinegar
500g (1lb 2oz) pork tenderloin
2tsp olive oil
½ tsp sea salt
½ tsp freshly ground black pepper
For the Gingered Peach Salsa:
3 medium-sized, just-ripe peaches
½ a red pepper, finely chopped
2 spring onions, finely chopped
2tbsp fresh lime juice
1tbsp grated ginger
1 clove garlic, finely chopped
½ tsp sea salt
2tbsp chopped fresh coriander

1 Preheat the oven to 200°C, Gas 6.
2 In a saucepan, bring the vinegar to a simmer and allow to reduce by half or until slightly syrupy. Set aside.
3 Using a sharp knife, trim any excess fat and sinew from the tenderloin.
4 Rub the pork all over with olive oil and sprinkle with salt and pepper. Heat a cast-iron baking dish on the hob over a high heat and brown the tenderloin on all sides. Remove from the heat and brush the tenderloin with all of the reduced vinegar.
5 Place in the oven for about 10–15 minutes or until a meat thermometer reaches 68°C, or the pork feels just firm and has only a hint of pink inside. Let it stand for 5 minutes before slicing. Serve with peach salsa below.
6 To make the salsa: Dip the peaches in boiling water for 20 seconds. Drain and run under cold water to cool, then skin, stone and chop. In a bowl, stir together the peaches, red pepper, onion, lime juice, ginger, garlic, salt and coriander. Cover and chill until needed, for up to 6 hours.

Serves 4

PORK AND PRAWN STIR FRY

180g (6oz) wholemeal
  spaghettini or vermicelli
1tbsp vegetable oil
250g (9oz) thinly sliced crisp
  green cabbage
1 onion, sliced
1 red pepper, sliced
2 cloves of garlic, finely chopped
1tbsp grated fresh ginger
180g (6oz) raw peeled prawns,
  de-veined
180g (6oz) Chinese-style Pork
  (see page 83), cut in
  matchsticks
1tsp hot chilli paste or powder
5tbsp Hoisin Glaze (see page 83)
2 spring onions, sliced diagonally

1 In a large pot of boiling salted water, cook the spaghettini for 6 minutes or until *al dente*. Drain and rinse with cold water. Set aside.
2 In a wok or large nonstick frying pan, heat 2tsp oil over a medium-high heat. Stir-fry the cabbage, onion, red pepper, garlic and ginger until just tender, about 5 minutes. Transfer the vegetables to a bowl and set aside.
3 In the same wok, heat the remaining oil over a high heat. When the oil is hot, add the prawns and stir-fry until opaque, about 2–3 minutes. Toss in the pork, then add the noodles, vegetables, chilli paste and Hoisin Glaze. Heat through, about 1 minute, tossing to coat the mixture with the sauce. Sprinkle each serving with the spring onions.

Variations: You can eliminate the noodles and serve the stir-fry over basmati rice. Just reduce the amount of Hoisin Glaze to 3tbsp.

Serves 4–6

PORK MEDALLIONS DIJON

2 pork tenderloins, about
  350g (12oz) each
3tbsp wholemeal flour
1/2tsp each sea salt and freshly
  ground black pepper
2tbsp olive oil
For the sauce:
2 onions, thinly sliced
1 clove of garlic, finely chopped
2tbsp wholemeal flour
3–4tbsp Dijon mustard
300ml (1/2 pint) skimmed milk
120ml (4fl.oz) dry white wine
1/4tsp each sea salt and
  freshly ground black pepper
1tbsp chopped fresh tarragon

1 Slice the pork into 2cm (3/4-inch) medallions. Place between 2 pieces of nonstick baking parchment and, using a meat mallet or rolling pin, beat to about 5mm (1/4-inch) thickness.
2 On a dinner plate, mix together 3tbsp flour and seasoning then press in the pork to coat, shaking off any excess. In a large nonstick frying pan, heat one tbsp of the oil over a medium-high heat. Cook the pork until golden brown on both sides, about 5–7 minutes; remove to a plate.
3 To make the sauce: In the same pan, add the remaining tbsp oil over a medium heat. Cook the onions and garlic, stirring often, for 5 minutes or until softened. Reduce the heat to medium-low and cook, stirring occasionally, for 10 minutes or until golden. Add 2tbsp flour and stir to coat the onions. Add the mustard and cook for 2 minutes. Stir in the milk, wine, salt and pepper. Cook, stirring constantly, until thickened. If mixture is too thick, stir in 1tbsp warm water. Stir in the tarragon and check the seasoning.

Serves 6

CHINESE-STYLE PORK WITH HOISIN GLAZE

This is such a versatile recipe. You can serve two with this recipe and save the rest to make the stir-fry on page 82, and then use the leftovers to make a delicious sandwich by stuffing sliced pork drizzled with glaze and topped with shredded lettuce or spinach in a wholemeal pitta or wrapped in a tortilla.

1 large pork tenderloin, about 400–500g
   (14oz–18oz)
4tbsp soy sauce
4tbsp Hoisin sauce
1 clove garlic, finely chopped
1tbsp sugar substitute or honey

1tbsp mirin or dry sherry
1tsp sesame oil
1tsp Chinese spice mixture (see below) or
   Chinese 5 Spice
1tsp vegetable oil
150ml (1/4 pint) chicken stock

1 Carefully cut small slashes in the pork so the marinade can penetrate the meat. In a medium bowl, whisk together the soy sauce, Hoisin sauce, garlic, sugar substitute or honey, mirin, sesame oil, and Chinese spice. Add the pork to the marinade and rub all over to coat well. Cover and chill for 24 hours, turning the pork a few times as it marinates.

2 Heat the oven to 190°C, Gas 5. Remove the pork from the marinade, wiping off any excess. Reserve the marinade. Heat a large frying pan over a high heat. Add the canola oil and swirl to coat the pan. Add the pork and sear until golden brown on all sides, about 2 minutes. Remove the pork to a rack set over a shallow roasting pan. Roast the pork in the top third of the oven for 15

minutes or until a meat thermometer registers 65°C when inserted in the centre of the tenderloin. (The pork can be cooled, wrapped well and chilled for up to 3 days.)

3 To make the glaze: In a small saucepan, mix the reserved marinade and stock. Bring to the boil over a medium-high heat. Reduce the heat so the marinade is simmering gently and cook until the mixture is reduced and thickened to a syrupy consistency, about 6–8 minutes. (The glaze can be cooled and refrigerated in an airtight container for up to 3 days.)

4 To serve, slice the pork thinly and drizzle with glaze.

Serves 4–6

CHINESE SPICE MIX (Makes about 2 tablespoons)

10 whole cloves
10 cardamom pods
1tsp coriander seeds
1tsp fennel seeds
1/2 tsp black peppercorns

1tsp cumin seeds
1/2 tsp ground ginger
1/4 tsp ground cinnamon
1/4 tsp ground turmeric

1 In a dry frying pan over a low heat, toast the cloves, cardamom, coriander, fennel, peppercorns and cumin seeds, stirring frequently, for 5 minutes or until the spices are

fragrant and starting to pop (be careful not to burn). Stir in the ground spices. Transfer to a spice grinder and grind finely. Keep for up to 3 months in an airtight container.

BLANQUETTE DE VEAU

A classic French bistro dish. Perfect to warm you up on a cold winter's night.

2tbsp olive oil
500g (1lb 2oz) lean boneless veal cut into 2cm (1-inch) pieces
750ml (1 ½ pints) chicken stock
120ml (4fl.oz) dry white wine
1 carrot, halved and sliced crosswise into 1cm (½-inch) pieces
1 stick celery, chopped
2tsp chopped fresh thyme
1 clove garlic, finely chopped
1 bay leaf
300g (10oz) baby onions, peeled (see tip below)
1tbsp soft margarine, preferably non-hydrogenated
180g (6oz) button mushrooms, quartered
1tbsp lemon juice
2tbsp cornflour
125g (4oz) low-fat natural yogurt
2tbsp chopped fresh parsley
Sea salt and freshly ground black pepper

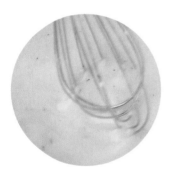

1 In a large heavy saucepan, heat 1tbsp oil over a medium-high heat. Lightly brown the meat on all sides. Add 500ml (18fl.oz) stock, the wine, carrot, celery, thyme, garlic and bay leaf. Bring to a simmer and cook, covered, for 20 minutes or until the meat is tender.

2 Meanwhile, in a small frying pan, cook the onions in the remaining stock, covered, for 15 minutes or until they are tender and the stock is absorbed. Remove from the heat and set aside.

3 In a nonstick frying pan, heat the remaining olive oil and margarine over a medium-high heat. Cook the mushrooms for 5 minutes or until softened. Stir in the lemon juice. Remove from the heat and set aside.

4 Using a slotted spoon, remove the meat and vegetables from the broth to a bowl. Discard the bay leaf. In a small bowl, blend the cornflour with 3tbsp broth; whisk back into the broth in a saucepan and cook, stirring, over a medium-high heat until thickened and smooth. Reduce the heat and stir in the yogurt. Return the meat and vegetables to the pot along with the reserved onions and mushrooms. Stir in the parsley. Season and serve.

Tip: To peel baby onions, cover them with boiling water and let stand for 2 minutes. Plunge into cold water and slip off the skins.

Serves 4

OSSO BUCCO WITH CAMPARI
AND ORANGE GREMOLATA

6 veal shanks, osso bucco cut,
  180–225g (6–8oz) each
2tbsp wholemeal flour
1/2 tsp each sea salt and freshly
  ground black pepper
3tbsp olive oil
1 onion, chopped
2 carrots, chopped
1 stick celery, chopped
3 cloves garlic, finely chopped
2 sprigs fresh thyme

3 sprigs fresh parsley
200ml (7fl.oz) dry white wine
3tbsp Campari*
2x400g cans chopped tomatoes
250ml (9fl.oz) beef stock
1/4 of an orange (with skin)
2 bay leaves
For the Gremolata:
4tbsp chopped fresh parsley
1 clove garlic, crushed
2tsp finely grated orange zest

1 Heat the oven to 190°C, Gas 5. Season the shanks with salt and pepper. Toss with the flour and shake off any excess.

2 In an ovenproof pot large enough to hold the meat in a single layer, heat 1tbsp oil over a medium-high heat. In 2 batches, brown the shanks well on all sides, then transfer to a plate.

3 Reduce the heat to medium and add the remaining 2tbsp olive oil to the pot along with the onion, carrot, celery, garlic, thyme and parsley. Cook, stirring, until the onions are golden and vegetables are starting to soften, about 10 minutes. Add the wine and Campari, stirring to loosen any brown bits on the bottom of the pan. Add the tomatoes, beef stock, orange and bay leaves. Return the shanks to the pot in a single layer and bring to a simmer. Cover the pot and braise in the centre of the oven, basting every 20 minutes and turning once, for 2 hours or until the meat is very tender when pierced with a fork.

4 To make the Gremolata: In a small bowl, stir together the parsley, garlic and orange zest. (This can be made several hours ahead, then covered and chilled.)

5 Remove the shanks from the pot, place on a plate and cover with foil to keep warm. Return the pot with the braising liquid to the heat and remove the orange, bay leaves, parsley and thyme stems. Bring the liquid to the boil and reduce a little to concentrate the flavour. Taste and adjust seasoning.

6 Place a portion of veal on a plate or shallow bowl. Ladle the braising liquid and vegetables over. Sprinkle with Gremolata.

*Campari adds a wonderful herbal quality but if not available use additional wine.

The traditional accompaniment to osso bucco is saffron risotto. To make a Gi version, use the barley risotto recipe on page 100 with the following changes: substitute 1 onion, chopped, for the leek, delete the lemon and Parmesan cheese and add 1/4 tsp crumbled saffron threads along with the stock.

Serves 6

BLUEBERRY BEEF BURGERS

The addition of blueberries helps to make these burgers moist and juicy.

A little vegetable oil
85g (3oz) blueberries
1tbsp balsamic vinegar
1tbsp Dijon mustard
1tsp Worcestershire sauce
2 cloves garlic, finely chopped
½tsp sea salt

¼tsp freshly ground black pepper
85g (3oz) ground flaxseeds
25g (1oz) porridge oats
500g (1lb 2oz) extra-lean minced beef
2 wholemeal buns
4 lettuce leaves
1 beef tomato, sliced in 4

1 Preheat the grill or a griddle pan to medium-high. Grease the grill rack or pan ridges with kitchen paper towel dipped in oil.

2 Blitz the blueberries with the vinegar, mustard, Worcestershire sauce, garlic, salt and pepper to a purée. Scrape into a large bowl. Stir in the flaxseeds and oats. Add the minced beef and mix with your hands or a wooden spoon until well combined.

3 Shape the mixture into four patties, each about 1cm thick. Place them on the greased grill or broiler pan and cook, turning once, until no longer pink inside, about 4–5 minutes per side. Serve each patty on half of a wholemeal bun. Top with the lettuce and tomato slices.

Serves 4

BOLOGNESE MEAT SAUCE

This is a great staple sauce to have on hand. Freeze it in plastic freezer bags in 6 portions and place in the fridge overnight to defrost. Use in lasagne, serve with wholewheat pasta or mix in cooked kidney beans and serve over brown basmati rice.

1tbsp olive oil
1 onion, chopped
500g (1lb 2oz) lean minced beef
120ml (4fl.oz) skimmed milk
2 cloves of garlic, finely chopped
1 small red pepper, cored
    and chopped
1 small green pepper,
    cored and chopped
1 stick of celery, chopped

1 carrot, chopped
1tbsp dried oregano
1tsp sea salt
1/2 tsp freshly ground
    black pepper
250ml (9fl.oz) red wine or
    grape juice
4x400g cans chopped tomatoes
1tbsp chopped fresh basil

1 In a large pot or deep frying pan, heat the oil over a medium-high   heat. Cook the beef for about 8 minutes or until browned, stirring to break up. Pour in the milk and cook for another 2–3 minutes or until the milk is evaporated. Reduce the heat to medium.

2 Add the onion, garlic, red and green peppers, celery, carrot, oregano, salt and pepper; cook, stirring, for about 5 minutes or until the vegetables are softened. Pour in the wine and cook, stirring and scraping up any brown bits, for 1 minute or until the wine is evaporated.

3 Add the tomatoes and basil, then bring to the boil. Reduce the heat and simmer for about 45 minutes or until the sauce is thick and flavourful. Check for seasoning and serve.

Makes 1.5 litres

MARINATED STEAK

Perfect for a summer barbecue party, paired with a big green salad.

4tbsp soy sauce
4tbsp orange juice
3tbsp vegetable oil
3tbsp rice wine vinegar
2 cloves garlic, finely chopped
2tbsp grated fresh ginger
1tbsp Dijon mustard
500g (1lb 2oz) sirloin or rump steak, in one piece

1 In a shallow dish, whisk together the soy sauce, orange juice, oil, vinegar, garlic, ginger and mustard. Trim the steak of any fat and turn in the marinade to coat evenly. Cover and marinate in the refrigerator for at least 4 hours and up to 8 hours, turning the meat occasionally.
2 Preheat a grill or large ridged griddled pan to a medium heat. Remove the steak from the marinade and cook, turning once, for 8 minutes per side for medium-rare or until it is done to your taste. Transfer to a chopping board and stand for 5 minutes covered with a tent of foil. Slice thinly across the grain.

Serves 4

BEEF STROGANOFF

A classic dish, perfect for guests or a family dinner. Serve with boiled new potatoes or wholemeal pasta.

500g (1lb 2oz) sirloin or rump
   steak, cut into strips
½ tsp each sea salt and freshly
   ground black pepper
1tbsp olive oil
1tbsp soft non-hydrogenated
   margarine

3 shallots, chopped
250g (9oz) mushrooms, sliced
250ml (9fl.oz) beef stock
1tbsp tomato purée
1tsp Worcestershire sauce
1tsp dried mustard powder
150g tub low-fat natural yogurt

1 Sprinkle the steak strips with salt and pepper. In a large nonstick frying pan, heat the oil over a high heat. Add the meat in a single layer (working in batches if necessary) and cook until just brown on the outside, about 1 minute per side. Remove the meat to a plate and set aside.

2 In the same pan, melt the margarine over a medium-high heat. Add the shallots and cook until starting to soften, about 2 minutes. Add the mushrooms and cook until tender and all liquid has evaporated, about 8–10 minutes.

3 In a small bowl, whisk together the stock, tomato purée, Worcestershire sauce and mustard powder. Return the steak to the pan and pour the stock mixture over. Simmer until the liquid thickens, about 10–12 minutes. Stir in the yogurt and cook on a very low heat until heated through, making sure not to overheat, or it might curdle. Check seasoning and serve.

Serves 4

STEAK AND PEPPER SIZZLE

Marinate the beef in the morning or the night before and come home to a quick and easy dinner.

500g (1lb 2oz) rump, sirloin
   or rib-eye steak, trimmed of
   all visible fat and thinly sliced
1tbsp olive oil
2 onions, sliced
1 each red and green pepper,
   cored and sliced
For the marinade:
125ml (4fl.oz) red wine
2 cloves of garlic, finely chopped
1¹/₂tbsp tomato purée
1tbsp Dijon mustard
1tsp Worcestershire sauce
¹/₂tsp freshly ground
   black pepper
¹/₂tsp sea salt

1 For the marinade: In a bowl whisk together the red wine, garlic, tomato purée, mustard, Worcestershire sauce and seasoning. Add the steak strips, stirring to coat. Cover and chill for 6–24 hours.
2 In a large nonstick frying pan, heat the oil over a medium-high heat. Cook the onion and red and green peppers for 8 minutes or until just softened. Remove to a plate and cover to keep warm.
3 Add the steak and marinade to the pan; cook for 5 minutes, stirring, until the steak is browned and cooked until just tender.
4 Return the vegetables to a skillet and toss with meat and sauce. Serve immediately.

Serves 4

BEEF AND PASTA BOWS

300g (10oz) wholemeal farfelle
350g (12 oz) extra-lean beef mince
1 onion, chopped
2 cloves garlic, finely chopped
1 courgette, chopped
1 large carrot, chopped
1 red pepper, chopped
125g (4oz) button mushrooms,
   chopped
250ml (9fl.oz) red wine
4 medium tomatoes, chopped
250ml (9fl.oz) basic tomato sauce,
   see page 156
3tbsp chopped fresh parsley
2tbsp chopped fresh basil
Sea salt and black pepper

1 In a large pot of boiling water, cook the pasta until *al dente*, about 10 minutes; drain and set aside.
2 In a large nonstick frying pan, stir-fry the beef and onion over a medium-high heat until browned, about 8 minutes. Add the garlic, courgette, carrot, red pepper and mushrooms and cook, stirring occasionally, until the vegetables have softened, about 6 minutes. Add the red wine and cook until the liquid has evaporated.
3 Add the tomatoes, tomato sauce and seasoning; simmer for 5 minutes. Stir in the pasta, parsley and basil. Reheat and serve.

Serves 4–6

MEATLESS

SAVOURY BEANS AND APPLE

This was adapted from a recipe suggested by reader Nadia. Serve with brown basmati rice and salad for a comforting vegetarian meal. Leftovers are great for lunch wrapped in wholemeal flour tortillas.

1tbsp olive oil
1 onion, chopped
2 apples, peeled, cored and grated
2 carrots, grated
1 stick celery, chopped
2 cloves garlic, finely chopped
250ml (9fl.oz) vegetable stock
3tbsp tomato purée
2tbsp sherry or red wine vinegar
2tsp each chopped fresh thyme and oregano
2tsp dried mustard powder
1tsp ground cumin
¼tsp each sea salt and ground black pepper
800g (1lb 10oz) cooked kidney beans, (or 2x400g cans, drained)
Low-fat natural yogurt (optional), to serve

1 In a large, nonstick frying pan, heat the oil over a medium-high heat. Cook the onion, apples, carrots, celery and garlic for 10 minutes, or until softened.
2 In a bowl, whisk together the stock, tomato purée and vinegar, then add to the vegetable mixture in the frying pan. Stir in the beans, thyme, oregano, mustard powder, cumin, salt and pepper. Bring to the boil. Reduce heat, cover and simmer for 45 minutes. Serve with a dollop of yogurt, if liked.

How to cook dried kidney beans: In a large saucepan, cover 300g dried kidney beans with 1.5 litres (2 3/4 pints) of water and bring to the boil. Remove from the heat and let stand for 6 hours (or overnight). Drain, rinse and cover with another 1.5 litres of fresh water. Bring to the boil; lower the heat and simmer, partially covered, for 1–2 hours or until tender. Add water as needed to keep the beans covered. Drain and season lightly after cooking.

Serves 6

LENTIL AND BEAN BAKE

If you like you can stir in meat – try cooked shredded turkey or smoked chicken (look in the deli section of most supermarkets) – before putting in the baking dish. Serve with basmati rice or pasta.

180g (6oz) Puy or green lentils
1tbsp olive oil
1 onion, chopped
4 cloves garlic, chopped
2x400g cans chopped tomatoes
300g (10oz) curly kale, trimmed of stems and shredded
2tsp Cajun seasoning, or to taste
½tsp sea salt
1x400g can red kidney beans, drained and rinsed
100g (3½oz) grated reduced-fat Cheddar cheese

1 In a saucepan, cook the lentils in 750ml (3/4 pint) water for 20–30 minutes or until soft. Drain and set aside.
2 Meanwhile, heat the oil in a large nonstick frying pan over a medium-high heat; cook the onion and garlic until softened, about 5 minutes. Add the tomatoes, kale, Cajun seasoning and salt; cook, stirring occasionally, for 10 minutes or until the kale is just tender. Stir in the lentils and beans.
3 Spoon the mixture into a 23x33cm (9x13-inch) ovenproof baking dish and sprinkle the cheese evenly over the top. Bake in a 190°C, Gas 5 oven for 20 minutes until browned and bubbling.

If Cajun spice is not available, you can make your own by combining 2tsp each of ground cumin, dried basil, dried oregano, dried mustard, paprika, dried thyme, 1tsp chilli powder and ½tsp cayenne and salt. This will keep for 3 months in an airtight container.

Serves 6

BARLEY RISOTTO WITH LEEKS, LEMON AND PEAS

We are always on the lookout for tasty vegetarian dishes for our son Stephen and his wife Jamie. This one is a hit.

1tbsp olive oil
1 medium leek, white and
    light-green part only,
chopped
2 cloves garlic, finely chopped
½tsp chopped fresh thyme
200g (7oz) pearl barley
4tbsp dry white wine
    or vermouth
750–900ml (1¼ – 1½ pints)
    vegetable stock
1 lemon, grated zest and juice
125g (4oz) frozen and
    thawed peas
2tbsp grated fresh Parmesan
Sea salt and black pepper

1   In a saucepan, heat the oil over a medium-high heat; cook the leek, garlic and thyme, stirring, for 3 minutes or until softened. Stir in the barley until well coated.
2   Stir in the wine and cook, stirring until the wine is absorbed. Add 750ml (1¼ pints) stock and bring to a boil. Cover and reduce the heat to low; simmer, stirring occasionally, for 40–45 minutes or until the barley is tender. If needed, stir in a little more stock or hot water near the end of cooking time to maintain a creamy consistency.
3   Stir in the peas and cook for 2–3 minutes more, then add the lemon juice, lemon zest and Parmesan; season to taste and serve hot.

Serves 4–6

BUCKWHEAT (KASHA) BURGERS

You can serve these meatless burgers on half a wholewheat bun dressed with your favourite green-light burger toppings or on their own with salad.

500ml (18fl.oz) vegetable stock
150g (5oz) buckwheat grains
    (kasha)
2tbsp olive oil
2 onions, chopped
250g (9oz) mushrooms,
    finely chopped
2 cloves garlic, crushed
75g (3oz) porridge oats, finely
    ground (use a spice grinder or
    food processor) or fine
    oatmeal
1½ tbsp soy sauce
½ tsp freshly ground black
    pepper, or to taste

1   In a saucepan, bring the stock to the boil. Add the buckwheat; reduce the heat and simmer for 20 minutes or until the liquid is evaporated and grains are tender. Remove and cool.
2   Meanwhile, in a nonstick frying pan, heat the oil over a medium-high heat. Cook the onions, mushrooms and garlic for 10 minutes or until softened and the liquid is evaporated. Remove to a large bowl.
3   Stir in the buckwheat, ground oats, soy sauce and pepper.
4   Using your hands, shape the mixture into 6 patties, about 2cm (1-inch) thick. Place on a pre-heated nonstick griddle or in a nonstick frying pan and cook for 4–5 minutes per side until crisp.

Makes 6

QUINOA, BEAN AND VEGETABLE CHILLI

160g (5 ½oz) quinoa, rinsed and drained
500ml (18fl.oz) water
¼tsp sea salt, 2tbsp olive oil
1 leek, white and light-green parts
    only chopped
3 cloves garlic, crushed
3 sticks celery, chopped
1 each red and green pepper, cored and chopped
1 large carrot, chopped
1 large fresh red chilli, seeded and
    finely chopped
1tsp chilli powder or to taste

2tsp dried oregano
1tsp cocoa powder
1tsp ground cumin
1tsp paprika
½tsp ground cinnamon
½tsp each sea salt and ground black pepper
1x400g can red kidney beans, rinsed and drained
1x400g can pinto or borlotti beans,
    rinsed and drained
4x400g cans chopped tomatoes
4 spring onions, chopped
1x142ml pot light soured cream or 150ml
    (4½fl.oz) half-fat crème fraîche

1 In a nonstick frying pan over a medium heat, roast the quinoa for 5 minutes or until fragrant and beginning to pop. In a small saucepan, bring the water to the boil. Add the salt and roasted quinoa, then cover and simmer over a medium heat for 15–20 minutes or until the water has been absorbed. Remove from the heat and stir. Cover and set aside.

2 Meanwhile, in a large saucepan, heat the oil over a medium heat. Cook the leeks and garlic for 5 minutes, or until softened. Stir in the celery, red and green peppers, carrot, fresh chilli, chilli powder, oregano, cocoa, cumin, paprika, cinnamon and seasoning. Cook for 10 minutes, stirring often.

3 Stir in the beans and tomatoes; simmer, stirring occasionally, for 20 minutes or until the vegetables are soft. Stir in the quinoa and spring onions and cook for 2 minutes, or until heated through. Garnish each serving with a dollop of soured cream.

Serves 8

FALAFEL WITH YOGURT-MINT SAUCE

2x400g cans chickpeas, drained and rinsed
4 cloves garlic, finely chopped
1tsp hot pepper sauce
1 ½tsp ground cumin
1tsp sea salt
1 ½tbsp fresh lemon juice
25g (1oz) parsley sprigs
125g (4oz) wholemeal flour
4–5tbsp olive oil
Pitta breads, chopped tomatoes and lettuce, to serve
For the yogurt-mint sauce:
125g (4oz) low-fat natural yogurt
½ a cucumber, coarsely grated and squeezed dry
2 cloves garlic, finely chopped
1tsp dried mint
Sea salt and freshly ground black pepper

1 In a food processor, whiz together the chickpeas, garlic, hot pepper sauce, cumin, salt, lemon juice and parsley. Transfer the mixture to a bowl and stir in the flour.
2 Shape the mixture into 24 balls and flatten slightly.
3 Heat the oil in a nonstick frying pan over a medium-high heat. Fry the falafel for 2–3 minutes per side or until golden brown.
4 Serve 2 or 3 per serving in pitta bread with chopped tomatoes, lettuce and yogurt-mint sauce.
5 To make the yogurt-mint sauce: Simply mix all the ingredients together.

Makes 24

RATATOUILLE

1 medium aubergine, halved lengthwise and
   sliced diagonally 5mm (¼-inch) thick
4tbsp olive oil, 1 large onion, halved and sliced
1 red pepper, cored and sliced 5mm
   (¼-inch) thick
1 green pepper, cored and sliced 5mm
   (¼-inch) thick
1 medium courgette, sliced diagonally 5mm
   (¼-inch) thick

2tbsp red wine vinegar
2x400g cans plum tomatoes, drained (reserve
   4tbsp of can juices) and roughly chopped
3 cloves garlic, finely chopped, 1tbsp chopped
   fresh thyme
1tbsp chopped fresh rosemary
2tbsp chopped fresh parsley
1tbsp chopped fresh basil
sea salt and freshly ground black pepper

1 Place the aubergine slices on a baking sheet and lightly brush both sides with 2tbsp of the olive oil then season lightly. Heat a grill and cook both sides of the aubergine until lightly browned.

2 Meanwhile, heat the remaining olive oil in a heavy-based wide and shallow pan over a medium-high heat. Add the onion and cook until starting to turn golden, about 5 minutes. Add the red and green pepper and courgette and cook until softened and golden brown, stirring occasionally.

3 Stir in the grilled aubergines, vinegar, tomatoes (and reserved can juice), garlic, thyme and rosemary; simmer for 5 minutes. Adjust seasoning to taste then stir in the parsley and basil to serve.

Ratatouille keeps for 3 days, covered, in the fridge. It can also be frozen for up to 3 months.

Serves 8

VEGETABLE CASSOULET

This meatless version of a classic French dish is chock-full of roasted vegetables, garlic and herbs, and will still satisfy a hearty appetite.

300g (10oz) dried white haricot or navy beans
4 whole cloves
1 onion, peeled and cut in half
1.2 litres (2 pints) chicken stock
4 cloves of garlic, finely chopped
2 sprigs of fresh parsley
1 sprig of fresh thyme
1 bay leaf
100g (3½oz) fresh wholemeal breadcrumbs
1tbsp plus 4tsp olive oil
2 carrots, sliced into 1cm (½-inch) rounds
1 sweet potato, peeled and cut into 1cm (½-inch) chunks

250g (9oz) celeriac, peeled and cut into 1cm (½-inch) chunks
Sea salt and freshly ground black pepper
1 onion, chopped
1 stalk of celery, chopped
350g (12oz) Brussels sprouts, trimmed and halved
250g (9oz) mushrooms, roughly chopped
250ml (9fl.oz) dry white wine
3tbsp tomato purée
1tbsp chopped fresh rosemary
1tsp dried thyme
1tsp dried oregano

1 Cover the beans with 3 times their volume of water and soak for 8 hours or overnight. Drain

2 Push 2 cloves into each onion half. Place in a large saucepan along with the beans, stock, garlic, parsley and thyme sprigs and bay leaf. Bring to the boil, then cover and simmer for 1–1½ hours or until the beans are tender. Drain and place in a large bowl, reserving the cooking liquid. Discard the onion, bay leaf and thyme sprig.

3 In a bowl, toss together the breadcrumbs and 1tbsp olive oil, then set aside. Preheat the oven to 220°C, Gas 7.

4 In a bowl, combine the carrots, sweet potato and celeriac; toss with 2tsp olive oil and a pinch each of salt and pepper. Arrange in an even layer on a rimmed baking sheet and roast for 25 minutes or until golden brown but still firm. Set aside.

5 In a large nonstick frying pan, heat the remaining 2tsp olive oil over a medium-high heat. Cook the chopped onion, celery, Brussels sprouts and mushrooms, stirring occasionally,

for 10 minutes or until the vegetables are softened. Stir in the wine, tomato purée, rosemary, thyme, oregano and seasoning. Cook for 2 minutes, then stir into the beans.

6 Reduce the oven heat to 180°C, Gas 4. In a large (4-litre capacity) casserole, spread half of the bean mixture. Top with the roasted vegetables, then the rest of the bean mixture. Pour in the reserved cooking liquid. Bake, uncovered, for 45 minutes. Remove from the oven and sprinkle the breadcrumb mixture evenly over the top. Return to the oven and continue cooking for another 45 minutes or until the topping is golden and the bean mixture is bubbling.

Tip: You can cook the beans a day ahead, chill them, then assemble the rest of the dish the next day.

Meat Variation: Stir in 250g (9oz) lean ham, chopped, into the bean mixture in Step 5.

Serves 6–8

AUBERGINE ROLLS WITH TOMATO SAUCE

This is a truly Mediterranean-flavoured dish. The combination of sun-dried tomatoes, mushroom, aubergine, basil and cheese will please everyone and the bulgur adds fibre and protein.

5tbsp olive oil
1 onion, chopped
2 cloves garlic, finely chopped
125g (4oz) mushrooms, chopped
200g (7oz) bulgur wheat
4 sun-dried tomatoes, chopped
500ml vegetable stock
125g (4oz) soft goats' cheese
2 medium-sized aubergines, about 550g (1–1 1/4 lb) each
1 litre (1 3/4 pints) basic tomato sauce (see page 156)
4tbsp chopped fresh basil
Sea salt and freshly ground black pepper

1 Heat 2tbsp oil in a large frying pan over a medium-high heat; cook the onion, garlic and mushrooms until softened, about 5 minutes.
2 Add the bulgur wheat and sun-dried tomatoes; stir until coated. Add the stock and bring to the boil, then reduce the heat and simmer, covered, for 20 minutes or until the liquid is absorbed. Transfer to a mixing bowl, cool and stir in the goats' cheese.
3 Meanwhile, peel 5cm (2-inch) wide strips of skin from opposite sides of the aubergines and discard, then cut each aubergine lengthwise into 6 slices, about 8mm (1/3-inch) thick. Brush both sides of the slices with the remaining olive oil and season lightly.
4 Preheat the grill to a medium heat and grill the slices, turning once, until softened, about 10 minutes. Transfer to a tray and set aside. Preheat the oven to 190°C, Gas 5.
5 Lay a slice of aubergine on your work surface and spread with 2–3tbsp bulgur mixture using a nonstick or wet spatula. Roll up from the narrow end and place, join-side down, on a tray. Repeat with the remaining aubergine and bulgur.
6 Pour the tomato sauce into a 23x32cm (9x13-inch) ovenproof baking dish. Place the aubergine rolls on top, seam-side down. Cover with foil and bake for 20 minutes, or until the sauce is bubbling. Serve 2–3 rolls per serving with tomato sauce and sprinkled with chopped basil.

Serves 4–6

VEGETABLE CRUMBLE

1tbsp olive oil
1 onion, chopped
1 medium leek, sliced
   (white and light-green part only)
1 medium courgette, cut into 2cm (1-inch) slices
1 large carrot, cut into 2 cm (1-inch) pieces
125g (4oz) sweet potato, peeled and cut into
   2cm (1-inch) chunks
125g (4oz) mushrooms, quartered
1 stick celery, cut in 1cm (1/2-inch) slices
1/2 a red pepper, cored and cut into 2cm
   (1-inch) slices
1tbsp chopped fresh thyme
25g (1oz) wholemeal flour

1x200g can tomatoes, roughly chopped
250ml (9fl.oz) vegetable stock
125ml (4fl.oz) milk
4tbsp chopped fresh parsley
1/2 tsp sea salt
1/2 tsp freshly ground black pepper
For the topping:
3tbsp soft margarine
25g (1oz) plain flour
3tbsp wheat bran
75g (3oz) grated reduced-fat mild
   Cheddar cheese
50g (2oz) chopped mixed nuts
2tbsp sesame seeds

1 Preheat the oven to 190°C, Gas 5. In a large saucepan, heat the oil over a medium-high heat. Cook the onion and leek for 5 minutes or until softened. Add the courgette, carrot, sweet potato, mushrooms, celery, red pepper and thyme. Cook, stirring often, for 10 minutes.
2 Mix in the flour and cook for 1 minute.
3 Stir in the tomatoes, stock, milk, parsley and seasoning; bring to the boil. Reduce the heat, cover and simmer for about 15 minutes or until the vegetables are tender.
4 Meanwhile, in a bowl, combine the margarine, flour and wheat bran. Using your fingers, rub the ingredients together until the mixture is crumbly. Stir in the cheese, nuts and sesame seeds.

5 Spoon the vegetable mixture into a 2-litre (11/2-pint) shallow baking dish. Sprinkle the crumble mixture evenly over top.
6 Bake for 30 minutes or until the topping is crisp and golden and the vegetable mixture is bubbling.

Freezer Storage Tip: Add 2tbsp wholemeal flour to the filling in Step 1. After Step 4, wrap well and freeze for up to 1 month. Bake from frozen, increasing the cooking time by 30–45 minutes.

Serves 4–6

MORROCAN SPICED VEGETABLE RAGOUT

1tbsp olive oil
1 large aubergine, cut into 1cm (1/2-inch) chunks
1 large onion, sliced
3 cloves of garlic, finely chopped
2tsp grated fresh ginger
2tsp garam masala (see page 157)
1tsp ground paprika
1tbsp tomato purée
750ml (1 1/4 pints) vegetable stock
1/2 a cauliflower, trimmed into small florets

2 carrots, cut into 1cm (1/2-inch) slices
1 red pepper, cored and chopped
1x400g can chickpeas, drained and rinsed
100g (3 1/2 oz) dried apricots, snipped
25g (1oz) raisins
1/2 tsp each sea salt and freshly ground
   black pepper,
125g (4oz) black olives, pitted
3tbsp chopped fresh coriander

1 In a large saucepan, heat the oil over a medium-high heat. Cook the aubergine, onion, garlic, ginger, garam masala and paprika for 8 minutes or until softened. Stir in the tomato purée.

2 Add the stock, cauliflower, carrots, red pepper, chickpeas, apricots, raisins and seasoning. Cover and simmer for 15–20 minutes or until the vegetables are tender. Stir in the olives and coriander and serve.

Serves 4

FISH AND SEAFOOD

THAI RED CURRY PRAWN PASTA

Thai curries have much more subtle flavours than many of the Indian versions. The combination of curry spices, lime and fresh coriander are hallmarks of Thai food.

500g (1lb 2oz) large raw prawns, peeled and de-veined
1tsp Thai red curry paste
1tbsp olive oil
4 cloves garlic, finely chopped
2 large tomatoes, skinned, deseeded and chopped
180ml (6fl.oz) white wine
Zest and juice of 1 lime
2tbsp chopped fresh coriander
180g (6oz) wholemeal spaghettini or linguine
Lime wedges, to serve
Sea salt and freshly ground black pepper

1 In a bowl, toss the prawns with the curry paste until well coated. Cover and chill for at least 2 and up to 8 hours.
2 Heat the oil in a large nonstick frying pan over a medium heat. Add the garlic and cook just until it starts to turn golden, about 1–2 minutes. Add the tomatoes, wine and lime juice and zest; bring to the boil, reduce heat and simmer until the sauce reduces and thickens, about 8 minutes.
3 Add the prawns and cook, stirring, until they are pink and firm, about 3–4 minutes; season to taste and stir in the coriander.
4 Cook the pasta in boiling salted water until al dente, about 8 minutes. Drain and add the pasta to the prawn mixture. Toss to coat and serve with the lime wedges.

Serves 4

SALMON, RED POTATO AND ASPARAGUS SALAD

This is a very attractive salad and perfect for serving at a spring or summer lunch party.

250g (9oz) skinless salmon fillet
5tbsp olive oil, preferably extra virgin
½tsp sea salt
½tsp freshly ground black pepper
250g (9oz) asparagus, ends trimmed and cut diagonally
into 2.5cm (1-inch) pieces
250g (9oz) new potatoes, preferably red-skinned, cooked and quartered
500g (1lb 2oz) cherry tomatoes, cut in half
125g (4oz) reduced-fat feta cheese, crumbled
6 spring onions, chopped
4tbsp chopped fresh mint
3tbsp chopped fresh basil
3tbsp chopped fresh dill
300g (10oz) mixed salad leaves or baby spinach
3tbsp lemon juice, 1tsp lemon zest
½tsp sea salt
¼tsp freshly ground black pepper

1 Brush the salmon with 1tbsp olive oil, then sprinkle with salt and pepper. Place the salmon on a greased grill over a medium-high heat and grill, turning once, until it is opaque and flakes easily with a fork, about 4 minutes per side. Remove to a plate and cool to room temperature. (Alternatively, bake the salmon at 220°C, Gas 7 for 10–12 minutes until opaque and flakes easily with a fork.)
2 In a steamer basket placed over a pan of boiling water, cook the asparagus, covered, until just tender, about 5 minutes. Rinse the asparagus under cold water until cool and set aside.
3 Make the vinaigrette by whisking together the remaining olive oil, lemon juice, zest and seasoning. Toss the salad leaves with 2tbsp of dressing and arrange on a large platter.
4 Break the salmon into bite-sized chunks and place in a large bowl. Add the potatoes, asparagus, tomatoes, feta, spring onions and fresh herbs; carefully toss with the remaining dressing. Spoon over salad and serve.

Serves 4–6

GRILLED TILAPIA WITH BLACK BEAN MANGO SALSA

4 tilapia fillets, about 125g (4oz) each
1tbsp olive oil, ½tsp ground cumin
½tsp each sea salt and ground black pepper
¼tsp cayenne pepper
For the salsa:
150g (5oz) cooked black beans
   (see cooking instructions below)
1 large ripe mango, diced

1 red pepper, finely chopped
Grated zest and juice of 1 lime
3tbsp chopped red onion
3tbsp chopped fresh mint
3tbsp chopped fresh coriander
2tsp chopped fresh chilli pepper or 2tsp hot
   chilli sauce
1tbsp extra-virgin olive oil,
A pinch each sea salt and ground black pepper

1 Pat the fillets dry using paper towel. Brush the oil over both sides of the fish. In a small bowl, mix together the cumin, salt, pepper and cayenne. Rub the spice mixture onto the fish.
2 Place the fillets on a hot greased griddle or under a medium-high grill. Cook for about 10 minutes, turning carefully once, or until fish is opaque and flakes easily with a fork. Let stand for 5 minutes before serving.
3 To make the salsa: In a bowl, stir together all the ingredients. Spoon over the fish to serve.

4 How to cook dried black beans: In a large saucepan, cover 180g (6oz) dried black beans with 1 litre (1 3/4 pints) of cold water and bring to the boil. Remove from the heat and let stand for 6 hours (or overnight). Drain, rinse and cover with 1 litre (1 3/4 pints) of fresh water. Bring to the boil, then lower the heat and simmer, partially covered, for 1½ hours or until tender. Add extra water as needed to keep the beans covered. Do not add salt while cooking, as it toughens the beans; season after. Beans can be frozen, in 3 or 4 batches, for up to 6 months.

Serves 4

MISO CRUSTED SALMON

1 clove of garlic, crushed
2tbsp white miso
1tbsp tahini
2tsp rice vinegar
1tsp mirin or sweet sherry
500g (1lb 2oz) fresh
   salmon fillet

1 Preheat the oven to 220°C, Gas 7. In a small bowl, whisk together the garlic, miso, tahini, rice vinegar and mirin.
2 Spread the miso mixture evenly over the surface of the salmon. Bake for 10–12 minutes or until the salmon flakes easily with a fork. Let stand for 5 minutes then serve.

Serves 4

BOUILLABAISSE WITH RED PEPPER ROUILLE

There is an actual Bouillabaisse Charter that states what ingredients can be used in the traditional Marseilles fish stew. This version takes some liberties, but is hearty and tasty nonetheless. It's a great dish for entertaining.

2tbsp olive oil
2 onions, chopped
½ a fennel bulb, chopped
1 medium carrot, chopped
2 sticks celery, chopped
1 large leek, chopped
4 cloves garlic, finely chopped
180ml (6fl.oz) white wine
2tbsp Pernod
3 plum tomatoes, chopped
1tbsp tomato puréé
2 bay leaves
1 sprig fresh thyme
1x3cm (1-inch) strip orange zest
1tsp saffron threads, crumbled
1tsp sea salt
½tsp freshly ground black pepper

1.5 litres (2 ½ pints) light fish or chicken stock
300g (10oz) Mediterranean-style firm-fleshed fish fillets, e.g. red snapper, red mullet, monkfish, bass, gurnard etc., cut in chunks
24 clams, scrubbed
36 mussels, scrubbed and beards removed
250g (9oz) large peeled prawns, de-veined
3tbsp chopped fresh parsley

For the Red Pepper Rouille:
1 red pepper
2 slices wholemeal bread, crusts removed and torn in pieces
2 cloves garlic, minced
Pinch each of salt and pepper
5–6tbsp extra-virgin olive oil

1 In a large cast-iron casserole or heavy-based saucepan, heat the oil over a medium heat; cook the onion, fennel, carrot, celery, leek and garlic until softened, about 8 minutes. Stir in the wine, Pernod, tomatoes, tomato purée, bay leaves, thyme, orange zest, saffron, salt and pepper; cook for 2 minutes.
2 Add the stock and bring to the boil. Simmer, uncovered, for 30 minutes or until the level is reduced by about 5cm (2 inches).
3 Meanwhile, make the Red Pepper Rouille: Quarter the pepper, remove the seeds and core, then place under a hot grill until the skin blackens. Peel off the skin. Place in a food processor with the bread, garlic, saltand pepper. With the machine running, pour in the olive oil

in a thin steady stream until creamy. If too thick, thin with a little warm water.
4 Now add the fish chunks, mussels and clams to the pot, stirring gently; cover and cook for 5 minutes. Add the prawns and cook for a further 5 minutes or until the fish is opaque, the prawns are pink and the mussels and clams have opened.
5 Discard any mussels and clams that do not open. Gently stir in the parsley. Using a slotted spoon, divide the fish and seafood evenly among warmed bowls. Ladle over the broth and vegetables and serve drizzled with a spoonful of Rouille.

Serves 6

DRUNKEN SALMON

120ml (4fl.oz) Scotch whisky
120ml (4fl.oz) freshly squeezed orange juice
4tbsp soy sauce
5–6tbsp olive oil
1tbsp freshly ground black pepper
2 cloves garlic, crushed
1kg (2¼lb) salmon fillet, skin on

1 Whisk together the whisky, orange juice, soy sauce, olive oil, pepper and garlic and tip into a baking dish, about 23x32cm (9x13 inch). Place the salmon fillet in the marinade, skin-side up. Cover with clingfilm and chill for 6–8 hours.
2 Preheat a grill or barbecue. Remove the salmon from the marinade and place skin-side down in the rack. Cook over a medium-high heat for 10–13 minutes, (if using a barbecue, cover with the lid) or until salmon just flakes with a fork. Be careful not to overcook.

Serves 8

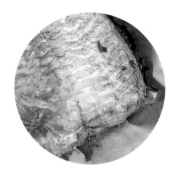

TUNA SALAD

1x400g can cannellini beans, drained and rinsed
1 clove garlic, finely chopped
2x185g cans tuna, drained
1 large tomato, chopped
3tbsp capers
1tbsp fresh lemon juice
2tbsp chopped fresh parsley
4 slices wholemeal bread
Sea salt and freshly ground black pepper

1 In a bowl, using a potato masher or large fork, mash or crush half the
  cannellini beans with the garlic.
2 In another large bowl, flake the tuna and mix with the tomato, capers,
  lemon juice and parsley. Stir in the bean mixture and season to taste.
3 Divide the mixture evenly among the slices of bread and serve as open
  sandwiches – or scoop into chicory or 'little gem' lettuce leaves.

Serves 4

CORNMEAL-MUSTARD SCALLOPS WITH SPINACH AND BEANS

2–3tbsp coarse-grained
    mustard
50g (2oz) cornmeal or polenta
500g (1lb 2oz) shelled scallops
2tsp olive oil
5tbsp chicken stock
1x400g can cannellini beans,
    drained and rinsed
2 cloves garlic, finely chopped
300g (10oz) baby spinach
1tbsp lemon juice
Pinch each of sea salt and
    freshly ground black pepper

1 In a bowl, combine the mustard and cornmeal.
2 Pat the scallops dry using paper towels. Add to the cornmeal mixture and coat well on all sides.
3 In a large nonstick frying pan, heat the oil over a medium-high heat. Sear the scallops on all sides, turning carefully, until the coating is golden and crisp, about 2 minutes in total. Do not overcook or the scallops will toughen. Remove to a plate; cover and place in a low oven to keep warm. Leave any remaining cornmeal coating in the pan.
4 In the same pan, add the stock, beans and garlic. Cook, stirring, for 2 minutes. Add the spinach and cook, stirring, for 3 minutes or until the spinach is wilted. Stir in the lemon juice and seasoning. Divide the spinach mixture among 4 plates and top with the scallops.

Serves 4

MUSSELS PROVENÇAL

Serve this easy but elegant dish, full of the flavour of southern France, with a simple green salad.

1.8kg (4lb) mussels
1tbsp olive oil
2 shallots, chopped
4 cloves of garlic, finely
    chopped
2tsp fennel seeds
2x400g cans chopped tomatoes
350ml (12fl.oz) dry white wine
1/2 tsp each sea salt and freshly
    ground black pepper
3–4tbsp chopped fresh parsley

1 Scrub the mussels under running water; trim off any beards. Discard any with cracked shells and any that do not close when tapped. Set aside.
2 In a large heavy saucepan, heat the oil over a medium-high heat. Cook the shallots and garlic for 5 minutes or until softened. Add the fennel seeds and tomatoes, and cook for 5 minutes. Stir in the wine and seasoning, and bring to the boil. Add the mussels and cook, covered, for 5 minutes or until the mussels open. Discard any that do not open. Serve in large bowls, sprinkled with parsley.

Serves 4

CITRUS-POACHED HADDOCK

Citrus fruits and fish seem to be made for each other. This is a quick and simple dish but elegant enough for company too.

1 small onion, finely chopped
1 clove of garlic, finely chopped
4tbsp fresh orange juice
4tbsp dry white wine or
   vermouth
1tbsp lemon juice
1tsp grated lemon zest
4tbsp fish, chicken or
   vegetable stock
500g (1lb 2oz) skinless, boneless
haddock fillet, cut into 4
2tbsp chopped fresh parsley
   or dill
Sea salt and freshly ground
black pepper

1 In a large frying pan, bring the onion, garlic, orange juice, wine or vermouth, lemon juice and zest to a boil, then simmer until the onions are softened and the liquid is reduced by half, about 5 minutes.
2 Add the stock and bring to the boil. Add the haddock, then reduce the heat and simmer gently, covered, for 10 minutes or until the fish flakes easily with a fork.
3 Using a slotted spoon, remove the haddock to a platter, cover and keep warm.
4 Return the pan juices to the boil and allow to reduce by a third. Stir in the parsley and season to taste. Pour the sauce over the fish and serve immediately.

Serves 4

GINGER-WASABI HALIBUT

This is also great on the barbecue. Serve with Cold noodle salad with cucumber and sesame (see page 53) for a refreshing summer meal.

2tbsp Dijon mustard
2tsp wasabi powder
3tbsp mirin or sweet sherry
2tbsp grated ginger
2tbsp chopped fresh coriander
4 fillets of halibut, about 125g
   (4oz) each

1 In a bowl, stir together the mustard and wasabi powder. Stir in the mirin, ginger and coriander. Place the fish in the marinade and turn to coat. Let it stand at room temperature for 20 minutes.
2 Preheat the oven to 180°C, Gas 4. Place the halibut on a baking sheet and bake for 8–10 minutes or until firm to touch. Let stand for 5 minutes then serve.

Serves 4

SNACKS

SPINACH BITES

This is great as a snack, hors d'oeuvre, or for lunch paired with a salad.

1tbsp olive oil
1 small onion, finely chopped
2 cloves garlic, minced
1 large fresh green chilli, seeded and finely chopped
350g (12oz) leaf spinach, chopped
1x250g tub low-fat cottage cheese
1 large egg
1tbsp grated fresh Parmesan
½tsp sea salt
¼tsp freshly ground black pepper
60g (2½oz) sunflower seeds, chopped
100g (3½oz) dried wholemeal breadcrumbs

1 In a large, nonstick frying pan, heat the oil over a medium-high heat. Cook the onion, garlic and chilli until softened, about 5 minutes. Add the spinach and cook, stirring, for another 5 minutes or until wilted and soft. Remove from the heat and set aside to cool.
2 In a large bowl, mix together the cottage cheese, egg and Parmesan. Season and stir in the spinach mixture until well combined. Stir in the sunflower seeds.
3 Heat the oven to 220°C, Gas 7. Cover a baking tray with a sheet of nonstick baking paper.
4 Place the breadcrumbs on a large plate. Scoop a tablespoon of mixture and place on top of the breadcrumbs. Cover with crumbs and gently form into a ball with your hands (the mixture will be slightly soft). Place on the baking sheet and repeat with the remaining mixture. Bake for 20 minutes or until golden and crisp.

Makes 20

BABA GHANOUSH

Here's a lighter but every bit as delicious version of a party-dip favourite. Serve with raw veggies or wholemeal pitta wedges.

1 large aubergine, about 750g (1 1/2 lb)
3 garlic cloves, finely chopped
5tbsp fresh lemon juice
4tbsp tahini
1/4 tsp ground cumin
1/2 tsp sea salt
1tbsp extra-virgin olive oil
1tbsp chopped fresh parsley
100g (3 1/2 oz) black olives, such as Kalamata

1 Heat the oven to 230°C, Gas 8. Prick the aubergine with a fork in several places and place on a greased grill over a medium-high heat. Grill, turning frequently, until the skin blackens and blisters and the flesh just begins to feel soft, about 10–15 minutes. Transfer the aubergine to a baking sheet and bake in the oven for 15–20 minutes or until very soft. Set aside until cool enough to handle. Peel off skin and discard.

2 Place the aubergine in a food processor. Add the garlic, lemon juice, tahini, cumin, and salt, then whiz until smooth. Add seasoning to taste. (If mixture is too thick, thin with a little water or more lemon juice to desired consistency.)

3 Transfer the mixture to a serving bowl and spread with the back of a spoon to form a shallow well. Drizzle the olive oil over the top and sprinkle with parsley. Arrange the olives around the side of the bowl and serve at room temperature.

Makes about 500g (1lb 2oz)

SMOKED SALMON AND DILL SCONES

125g (4oz) wholemeal flour
40g (1 ½oz) wheat bran
½tsp bicarbonate of soda
125g (4oz) smoked salmon,
    chopped
3tbsp chopped fresh dill
¼tsp each sea salt and ground
    black pepper
125g (4oz) low-fat
    natural yogurt
1x284ml pot buttermilk*
1 large egg, lightly beaten

1 Preheat the oven to 220°C, Gas 7. In a large bowl, combine the flour, bran, bicarbonate of soda and seasoning. Stir in the salmon and dill. Add the yogurt and just enough buttermilk to mix to make a soft, slightly sticky dough.
2 Turn the dough out onto a floured surface and knead gently 6 times, or until smooth. Pat out to 2cm (1-inch) thickness and cut the dough into 5cm (2-inch) rounds. Place on a baking sheet and brush the tops with beaten egg. Bake for about 15 minutes or until golden on the bottom.
3 Split and serve with Dill Cream (see below), if liked.

To make the Dill Cream: Take 125g (4oz) strained yogurt (see page 157), 3tbsp chopped fresh dill, 1tsp lemon juice and 1 clove garlic (crushed). In a bowl, stir together all the ingredients. Cover and chill for up to 2 days.

*if buttermilk is not available use 250ml skimmed milk plus 1tbsp (15ml) lemon juice or white vinegar. Let stand for 10 minutes.

Makes 12

WASABI CHICKPEAS

2x400g cans chickpeas, rinsed
    and well drained
2tbsp olive oil
1tbsp mustard powder
2tbsp rice vinegar
2tbsp wasabi powder
½tsp sesame oil
½tsp each sea salt and
    ground black pepper

1 Preheat the oven to 200°C, Gas 6. In a large bowl, whisk together the olive oil, mustard powder, rice vinegar, wasabi powder, sesame oil, salt and pepper. Stir in the chickpeas, tossing to coat well.
2 Spread the mixture in a single layer on a flat baking sheet lined with nonstick baking parchment paper. Bake for 40–45 minutes or until golden. Cool and store in an airtight container until required.

Makes 500g (1lb 2oz)

COLOURFUL VEGGIE TOFU SPREAD AND DIP

1x250g pack firm tofu
1 small carrot, grated
1/2 a red pepper, chopped
1 stick of celery, chopped
4tbsp roughly chopped parsley
2tbsp mild American-style
   mustard
2tbsp reduced-fat mayonnaise
2tsp soy sauce

1 In a food processor, blend together all the ingredients until smooth.

Storage: Keeps refrigerated, in an airtight container, for up to 5 days.

Makes about 450g (1lb)

BASMATI RICE CRACKERS

Best eaten freshly baked and perfect for serving with dips.

1tbsp olive oil
1/2 a medium onion, chopped
2 cloves garlic, finely chopped
150g (5oz) brown basmati rice
500ml (18fl.oz) chicken stock
1/4 tsp each sea salt and freshly
   ground black pepper

1 In a saucepan, heat the oil over a medium heat. Add the onion and garlic and cook for 2 minutes, or until softened. Add the rice, stock and salt, and bring to a boil. Reduce the heat to low, cover and cook for 45 minutes or until all the liquid is absorbed. Remove from the heat and let sit for 10 minutes. Remove to a bowl and allow to cool to room temperature.
2 Spoon the rice mixture out onto a large sheet of nonstick baking parchment and cover with another sheet of paper. Using a rolling pin, roll out into approximately a large rectangle, about the thickness of a £1 coin. Remove the top sheet of paper and, using a 5cm (2-inch) round cutter, cut out about 24 rounds.
3 Preheat the oven to 190°C, Gas 5. Carefully transfer the rounds to a baking sheet lined with nonstick baking parchment. Bake for 20–25 minutes until crisp and golden brown. Allow to cool completely on a rack.

Makes 20–25 crackers

RED LENTIL HUMMUS

A great dip for veggies or as a sandwich spread. Great with Basmati Rice Crackers (see recipe on page 131).

200g (7oz) split red lentils
6–8 sun-dried tomatoes, soaked in hot water, drained and snipped
3tbsp tahini
3 cloves garlic, finely chopped

¼tsp ground cumin
½tsp each sea salt and ground black pepper
3tbsp extra-virgin olive oil
1tbsp lemon juice

1 In a saucepan, bring 750ml (1¼ pints) water to a boil. Add the lentils and cook, uncovered, for 15–20 minutes, or until tender; drain if necessary.
2 In a food processor, pulse together the cooked lentils, sun-dried tomatoes, tahini, garlic, cumin, salt and pepper until smooth. With the food processor running, add the oil and lemon juice.

Storage: This will keep in an airtight container. refrigerated, for up to 2 days.

Smoky Version: Add ¼tsp smoked paprika along with cumin.

Makes 500g – enough for 8 servings

CARROT MUFFINS

125g (4oz) wholemeal flour
25g (1oz) wheat bran
50g (2oz) ground flaxseeds or linseeds
4tbsp sugar substitute
2tsp ground cinnamon
1tsp ground ginger
½tsp bicarbonate of soda
2tsp baking powder
¼tsp fine sea salt

2 eggs
250ml (9fl.oz) buttermilk*
4tbsp vegetable oil
1tsp vanilla extract
1 large carrot, finely grated
75g (3oz) raisins, softened in hot water for
   10 minutes and drained
40g (1½oz) pecans, chopped

1 Preheat the oven to 190°C, Gas 5. Line a 12-hole deep muffin tin with muffin paper cases or grease well.
2 In a large bowl, combine the flour, bran, flaxseed or linseed, sugar substitute, cinnamon, ginger, bicarbonate, baking powder and salt. In a small bowl, whisk together the eggs, buttermilk, oil and vanilla. Stir in the carrots, raisins and pecans. Add to the flour mixture and stir just until combined.

3 Spoon into the prepared tin and bake for 20–25 minutes or until a tester inserted in the centre of a muffin comes out clean.

Storage: Muffins can be kept at room temperature for about 2 days or wrap them well and freeze in a resealable plastic bag or airtight container for up to 1 month.

*If buttermilk is not available use 250ml skimmed milk plus 1tbsp (15ml) lemon juice or white vinegar. Let stand for 10 minutes.

CRANBERRY-ALMOND BISCOTTI

These biscotti are both delicious and attractive. The red cranberries make them great to serve at Christmas so bake lots, wrap them in a clear bag with a bow and give as gifts.

Juice and zest of 1 orange
1tbsp Amaretto liqueur
1x75g pack dried cranberries
250g (9oz) wholemeal flour
8tbsp sugar substitute
1tsp cinnamon
½tsp baking powder
½tsp bicarbonate of soda
¼tsp ground nutmeg
1 large egg
1 egg white
50g (2oz) toasted almonds, chopped

1 In a small saucepan, heat the orange juice, Amaretto and cranberries just until hot. Remove from the heat and let stand for 10 minutes. Drain and reserve the juice.
2 Preheat the oven to 180°C, Gas 4 and line a baking sheet with nonstick baking parchment.
3 In a large bowl, mix together the flour, sugar substitute, cinnamon, baking powder, bicarbonate of soda and nutmeg.
4 In a separate bowl, whisk together the egg, egg white, orange zest and 2tbsp reserved juice; stir into the dry mixture until combined, adding more juice if necessary to make the dough moist. Stir in the almonds and cranberries.
5 With lightly floured hands, shape into a 40cm (16-inch) log, then flatten slightly. Bake for 20 minutes or until firm. Slide onto a cooling rack and cool for 10 minutes while you reduce the oven to 160°C, Gas 2.
6 Cut the log diagonally into 1cm (½-inch) thick slices. Place on the baking sheet, leaving a 2–3cm (1-inch) space between each. Bake until golden brown and crunchy, about 25 minutes. Allow to cool on the rack.

Storage: The Biscotti can be stored in an airtight container for up to 1 week or wrapped and frozen for up to 3 months.

Makes about 20

ORANGE AND CRANBERRY BRAN MUFFINS

The cranberries give these moist muffins a nice little kick of tartness. They're perfect for a mid-morning snack.

25g (1oz) wheat bran
50g (2oz) All-Bran or Bran Flakes
120ml (4fl.oz) boiling water
1x284ml carton buttermilk*
5tbsp sugar substitute
4tbsp vegetable oil
1 large egg
1tbsp frozen orange juice concentrate, thawed
1tsp grated orange zest
1tsp vanilla essence,

150g (5oz) wholemeal flour
75g (3oz) ground flaxseeds or linseeds
1 1/2 tsp bicarbonate of soda
1tsp ground cinnamon
1/2 tsp ground ginger
1/4 tsp sea salt
150g (5oz) fresh or frozen cranberries, roughly chopped
25g (1oz) toasted pumpkin seeds (optional)

1 Preheat the oven to 200°C, Gas 6. In a large bowl, combine the bran and cereal. Stir in boiling water to moisten, then allow to cool for 5 minutes. Stir in the buttermilk, sugar substitute, oil, egg, orange juice, orange zest and vanilla essence.

2 In a separate large bowl, combine the flour, flaxseeds, bicarbonate, cinnamon, ginger and salt; mix in the cranberries, and pumpkin seeds, if using. Add to the bran mixture, stirring until just combined.

3 Divide the batter among 12 deep cup bun or muffin tins lined with paper cases (or lightly greased if nonstick) and bake for about 25 minutes or until a thin skewer inserted in the centre comes out clean.

To toast the pumpkin seeds: Place seeds in a dry pan, frying over a medium heat. Toast, stirring occasionally, for 5 minutes or until the seeds are popping and fragrant.

Storage: The muffins can be kept at room temperature for about 2 days or, if well wrapped and frozen in a resealable plastic bag or airtight container, for up to 1 month.

*if buttermilk is not available use 250ml skimmed milk plus 1tbsp (15ml) lemon juice or white vinegar. Let stand for 10 minutes.

Makes 12 muffins

STRAWBERRY TEA BREAD

Perfect for that afternoon cup of tea and the recipe makes two loaves: one for now and one for the freezer. It's so handy for unexpected guests. You can also serve it as a dessert with some sliced berries on the side.

250g (9oz) wholemeal flour
20g (3/4oz) wheat bran
150g (5oz) porridge oats
1tsp cinnamon
½tsp sea salt
1tsp bicarbonate of soda
½tsp baking powder
3 large eggs, beaten
12tbsp sugar substitute
120ml (4fl.oz) vegetable oil
120ml (4fl.oz) skimmed milk
1tsp vanilla essence
400g strawberries, fresh, crushed

1 Grease and line 2x1kg (2lb) loaf tins. Heat the oven to 190°C, Gas 5.
2 In a large bowl, stir together the flour, wheat bran, oats, cinnamon, salt, bicarbonate of soda and baking powder; set aside.
3 In a separate bowl, whisk together the eggs, sugar substitute, oil, milk and vanilla essence. Pour over the dry ingredients and stir just until moistened. Stir in the strawberries and divide between the loaf tins.
4 Bake in the centre of the oven for 45–50 minutes or until a thin skewer inserted in the centre comes out clean. Let the loaves cool in the pan on a rack for 15 minutes. Turn out onto rack and let cool completely.

Storage: Wrap in clingfilm or foil and store at room temperature for up to 3 days, or wrap in freezer film or a freezer bag, seal, label and freeze for up to 1 month.

Makes 2 loaves

BLUEBERRY ROCK CAKES

These little cakes make a very satisfying snack. You can replace the blueberries with blackcurrants or loganberries and adjust the sweetener. Using frozen fruit may turn the cakes blue, while fresh will not.

1 large egg
8tbsp sugar substitute
120ml (4fl.oz) skimmed milk
4tbsp vegetable oil
200g (7oz) wholemeal flour
50g (2oz) porridge oats
2tbsp wheat bran
2tbsp poppy seeds
1tbsp baking powder
½tsp lemon zest
½tsp cinnamon
½tsp sea salt
100g (3½oz) fresh blueberries

1 Preheat the oven to 190°C, Gas 5. Line a baking sheet with nonstick baking parchment.
2 In a large bowl, whisk together the egg, sugar substitute, milk and oil.
3 In another bowl, mix together the flour, oats, wheat bran, poppy seeds, baking powder, lemon zest, cinnamon and salt. Stir in the egg mixture just until combined. Gently mix in the blueberries.
4 Drop the batter in 8 mounds onto the lined baking sheet and bake for about 15–20 minutes until firm and golden brown. Remove to a cooling rack and cool.

Storage: These are best eaten the day they are made, but can be frozen in a plastic bag or freezer container for up to 1 month.

Makes 8 cakes

DESSERTS

CHOCOLATE PUDDING

Ruth loves chocolate and strawberries. This dessert is a favourite.

2tbsp cornflour or arrowroot
20g (3/4 oz) cocoa powder
2tbsp sugar substitute
1/4tsp sea salt
500ml (18fl.oz) skimmed
  milk
2tsp vanilla essence
125g (4oz) raspberries or
sliced strawberries, or a
  mixture (optional)

1 In a saucepan, stir together the cornflour, cocoa, sugar substitute and salt. Add the milk and vanilla essence and cook over a medium-high heat, stirring constantly until boiling and the mixture thickens. Continue cooking, stirring, for 3 minutes, then remove from the heat and stir in berries, if using.
2 Pour into a large serving bowl or 4 individual serving dishes. Cool to room temperature and chill before serving.

Storage: This will keep in the fridge for up to 2 days.

Serves 4

LEMON CRÈME FRAÎCHE ICE CREAM

350g (12oz) reduced-fat
  crème fraîche
350g (12oz) 0%-fat natural
  yogurt
8tbsp sugar substitute
Juice and grated zest of
  1 lemon

1 In a bowl, whisk together the crème fraîche, yogurt, sugar substitute, lemon juice and zest until the sugar substitute is dissolved. Pour into an ice-cream maker and churn until frozen. Then scoop into a freezer-proof container and freeze until required.
2 (Alternatively, pour the mixture into a medium-sized freezer container and freeze until firm, about 2 hours. Cut into chunks and, working in batches, place the frozen chunks in a food processor. Purée until smooth, scrape back into the container and freeze until firm.)
3 Before serving, place the ice cream in the fridge for at least 15 minutes to soften enough for scooping.

Serves 4–6

PANNA COTTA WITH BLUEBERRY SAUCE

Italian for 'cooked cream', this silky eggless custard is a refreshing end to
a meal. You can substitute blackberries for the blueberries if desired.

1tbsp gelatine crystals
500ml (18fl.oz) skimmed milk
1tsp vanilla essence
8tbsp sugar substitute
250ml (9fl.oz) buttermilk*
125g (4oz) 0%-fat thick or Greek natural yogurt

For the blueberry sauce:
250g (9oz) blueberries
120ml (4floz) grape juice
3tbsp sugar substitute
2tbsp Grand Marnier, optional

1 In a small bowl, sprinkle the gelatine over 3tbsp cold water, stir once then leave to soak for about 10 minutes (do not stir again).
2 Meanwhile, in a saucepan over a medium heat, bring the milk, vanilla essence and sugar substitute to a simmer, stirring occasionally to dissolve the sugar substitute. Remove from the heat and add the gelatin, stirring until completely dissolved and the mixture is smooth. Cool to room temperature, about 30 minutes.
3 Stir the buttermilk and yogurt into the milk mixture. Strain through a fine-mesh sieve and divide the mixture among 6 custard cups or ramekins. Chill until the panna cotta is set, 3–6 hours (it must be used within 24 hours).
4 To make the blueberry sauce, in a saucepan bring the blueberries, grape juice, sugar substitute and Grand Marnier, if using, to the boil over a medium-high heat. Continue to boil until the sugar substitute is dissolved and the berries are starting to burst.

5 Transfer half of the mixture to the bowl of a food processor and purée until smooth. Return to the mixture in saucepan and cook, stirring, for 2 minutes. Remove from the heat and cool to room temperature.
6 Demould the panna cotta by running a knife around the sides of each panna cotta to loosen and invert onto serving plates, shaking gently to release onto the plate. Spoon the blueberry sauce around and over the top of the panna cotta.

*if buttermilk is not available use 250ml skimmed milk plus 1tbsp (15ml) lemon juice or white vinegar. Let stand for 10 minutes.

Serves 6

FRUIT SALAD

You can substitute other types of fruit – just make sure they are mostly green-light.

250ml (9fl.oz) hot mixed fruit, berry or herbal tea
2tbsp fresh orange juice
1tsp sugar substitute or honey
1tsp vanilla essence
1tsp ground cardamom
250g (9oz) strawberries
2 kiwis
2 ripe pears
1 each orange and grapefruit
1x150g pack blueberries, blackberries or raspberries
1 large apple
1 banana
Seeds of half a pomegranate

1 Prepare the fruit: hull and halve the strawberries, peel and slice the kiwis and banana, core the pears and apple and cut into bite-sized chunks and peel and segment the orange and grapefruit.
2 In a small bowl, whisk together the hot tea, orange juice, sugar substitute, vanilla and cardamom. Cool to room temperature.
3 In a large bowl, mix together all the fruits and the pomegranate seeds, pour over the tea mixture, stir gently to mix, then serve.

Serving tip: Sprinkle the fruit with some sunflower and/or pumpkin seeds and serve with a dollop of yogurt or low-fat, no sugar added ice cream.

Serves 6–8

TOFU-ALMOND CHEESECAKE

The great thing about this cheesecake is there is no need for a long cooking time in a water bath.

For the base:
25g (1oz) ground almonds
40g (1½ oz) jumbo porridge oats
60g (1½ oz) wholemeal flour
5g (¼ oz) sugar substitute
4tbsp soft margarine, non-hydrogenated
For the filling:
2x250g packs firm tofu
15g (½ oz) sugar substitute
1x140g pot low-fat vanilla yogurt
2tbsp lemon juice
1tbsp almond essence
1 egg
2tsp vanilla essence
¼ tsp sea salt

1. For the base: preheat the oven to 180°C, Gas 4. In a bowl, mix together the almonds, oats, flour and sugar substitute. Rub in the margarine until the mixture is crumbly. Pat into the base of a 20cm (8-inch) spring-form pan. Bake for 15 minutes, or until firm, then remove and cool.
2. For the filling: purée all the ingredients in a food processor until smooth. Pour over the crust and return to the oven for 45 minutes or until the filling is set. Remove and run a knife around the edge to loosen. Allow to cool completely. Serve with fresh berries or berry filling from Berry-Stuffed French Toast (page 33).

Storage: Cover and chill for up to 2 days.

Serves 8–10

CARROT CAKE WITH CREAM CHEESE ICING

250g (9oz) wholemeal flour
2tsp baking powder
1tsp bicarbonate of soda
½tsp sea salt
2tsp ground cinnamon
½tsp ground ginger
¼tsp ground allspice
¼tsp ground cardamom, optional
¼tsp ground nutmeg
120ml (4fl.oz) olive oil
12tbsp sugar substitute
1tsp vanilla essence
2 eggs

4 carrots, grated
1 medium apple, cored and grated
125g (4oz) unsweetened apple sauce or purée
100g (3½oz) drained juice-packed
    crushed pineapple
60g (2½oz) toasted chopped walnuts (optional)
For the Cream Cheese Icing:
125g (4oz) light cream cheese
4tbsp strained yogurt (p. 157) or low-fat yogurt
1tbsp sugar substitute (or to taste)
1tbsp frozen orange juice concentrate
½tsp vanilla essence

1 Grease a 20–23cm (8–9-inch) round cake tin. Preheat the oven to 180°C, Gas 4. In a large bowl, mix together the flour, baking powder, bicarbonate of soda, salt and spices.

2 In a separate bowl, beat together the olive oil, sugar substitute and vanilla until smooth. Beat in the eggs, one at a time. Stir in the carrot, apple, apple sauce, crushed pineapple and walnuts, if using. Pour over the flour mixture and stir to mix. Spoon into a prepared tin.

3 Bake in the centre of the oven for 45–50 minutes or until a thin skewer inserted in the centre comes out clean. Let cool in the tin on a rack for 15 minutes. Run a knife around the edge of the cake and turn out onto a rack to cool completely.

4 In a bowl, beat together the cream cheese, yogurt, sugar substitute, orange juice concentrate and vanilla until smooth. Spread over the top and sides of the cake.

Storage: Wrap well and store at room temperature for up to 2 days, or freeze for up to 1 month. (When iced, cake can be chilled for up to 2 days.)

Serves 8–12

ONE-BOWL CHOCOLATE CAKE WITH GANACHE ICING

Many of our readers have requested a birthday or party cake, so here it is.

200g (7oz) wholemeal flour
12tbsp sugar substitute
40g (1½oz) cocoa powder
1½tsp bicarbonate of soda
1½tsp baking powder
½tsp sea salt
1 large egg
1 egg white
160ml (5½fl.oz) buttermilk*
1 small can unsweetened apple sauce (110ml/4fl.oz)
2tbsp vegetable oil
1tsp vanilla essence
Zest of 1 orange
For the Ganache Icing (Yellow light):
200g / 7oz dark chocolate, 70% cocoa solids
250ml / 9floz soya milk

1 Preheat the oven to 180°C, Gas 4. Grease a 20cm (8-inch) round deep cake or spring-form tin. Line the base with a round of baking parchment.
2 In a food processor or mixer, whiz together all ingredients just until smooth.
3 Pour the batter into the prepared tin, smoothing the top. Bake for 20–25 minutes or until the top springs back when lightly touched and a toothpick inserted in the centre comes out clean.
4 Allow to cool in the tin on a rack for 30 minutes, then demould from the tin and remove the parchment paper; let the cake cool completely on a rack. Serve in wedges, or split cake into 2 or 3 rounds, sandwich with ganache (see below), and smooth more over the top and sides.
5 For the Ganache Icing: Melt the chocolate in a bowl set over barely simmering water or in a microwave set on medium power. Remove from the heat and whisk in the soya milk until smooth. Cool and beat again before using.

Storage: Leftover ganache can be chilled for up to 3 days or frozen for 3 months. Melt in a bowl set over barely simmering water, cool and beat until smooth.

*if buttermilk is not available use 250ml skimmed milk plus 1tbsp (15ml) lemon juice or white vinegar. Let stand for 10 minutes.

Serves 6–8

APPLE UPSIDE-DOWN CAKE

This cake is just as delicious made with pears.

180ml (6fl.oz) apple juice
6 eating apples, peeled and sliced,
    e.g. Braeburn or Cox's
16tbsp sugar substitute
1tsp ground cinnamon
½tsp ground ginger
¼tsp ground cloves optional

For the cake:
60g (2¼oz) soft margarine,
    non-hydrogenated
12tbsp sugar substitute
1 large egg
1 egg white
1tsp vanilla essence
190g (6½oz) wholemeal flour
1tsp baking powder, 1tsp bicarbonate of soda
½tsp ground ginger
¼tsp sea salt
120ml (4fl.oz) buttermilk*

1 Grease the bottom and sides of a 23cm (9-inch) spring-form cake tin. Preheat the oven to 180°C, Gas 4.

2 In a large nonstick frying pan, heat the apple juice over a medium-high heat. Add the apples, sugar substitute, cloves, cinnamon and ginger; toss to combine. Continue to cook, stirring occasionally, for 6–8 minutes or until the liquid is absorbed and the apples have softened slightly. Pour the apples into the bottom of your prepared pan, spreading evenly. Set aside.

3 For the cake: In a bowl, beat the margarine with the sugar substitute until creamy; then beat in the egg and egg white separately, then the vanilla essence. In a separate bowl, mix together the flour, baking powder, bicarbonate, ginger and salt; stir half of this into the margarine mixture. Mix in buttermilk, then the remaining flour mixture.

4 Pour into your pan on top of the apples, spreading evenly. Bake in the centre of the oven for 40–45 minutes or until the top springs back when lightly touched. Allow to cool in the pan on a rack for 15 minutes, then demould onto a cake plate.

Serve warm with a scoop of low-fat, no sugar added ice cream or strained yogurt (page 157)

*if buttermilk is not available use 250ml skimmed milk plus 1tbsp (15ml) lemon juice or white vinegar. Let stand for 10 minutes.

Serves 6

OATMEAL CHOCOLATE CHUNK COOKIES

160g (5½oz) jumbo porridge oats
85g (3oz) wholemeal flour
25g (1oz) ground flaxseed
    or linseed
2tsp ground cinnamon
1tsp bicarbonate of soda
½tsp baking powder
¼tsp sea salt
125g (4oz) soft margarine,
    non-hydrogenated
8tbsp sugar substitute
1 egg
3tbsp water
2tbsp tahini
2tsp vanilla essence
50g (2oz) 70%-cocoa-solids
    chocolate, chopped

1 Preheat the oven to 180°C, Gas 4. In a large bowl, stir together the oats, flour, flaxseed, cinnamon, baking soda, baking powder and salt. Set aside.
2 In another bowl, beat the margarine, sugar substitute, egg, water, tahini and vanilla essence until smooth. Stir the oat mixture into the margarine mixture, then add the chocolate and stir to combine. Drop heaped teaspoonfuls onto a baking sheet lined with nonstick baking parchment and flatten slightly. Bake for 10–12 minutes or until firm. Allow to cool on a rack.

Storage: Keep in an airtight container for up to 3 days or freeze for up to 1 month.

Variation: You can substitute 100g (3½oz) dried currants, dried cranberries or chopped dried apricots for the chocolate.

Makes about 24 cookies

CREAMY RASPBERRY FOOL

No one will know this dessert is so easy to make. Serve it as is or dress it up with some fresh fruit or berries.

1x500g tub low-fat cottage
    cheese
250g (9oz) fresh or frozen
    and lightly thawed
    raspberries
4tbsp sugar substitute
1tbsp amaretto or berry-
    flavoured liqueur (optional)

1 In a blender or food processor fitted with a steel blade, process the cottage cheese, raspberries, sugar substitute and amaretto, if using.
2 Spoon immediately in 4 glass dishes, or cover and chill for up to 3 days.

Serves 4

PLUM CRUMBLE

Crumbles have to be the perfect green-light desserts. You can make them with an amazing combination of fruits – limited only by availability. For example, try pears instead of plums and cut back slightly on the sugar substitute but keep in the ginger. Use all sorts of different combinations and enjoy.

750g (1 ⅓ lb) plums, halved
1tbsp sugar substitute
1tbsp cornflour
½tsp ground ginger
½tsp ground cinnamon
For the topping:
75g (3oz) jumbo porridge oats
60g (2 ½oz) wholemeal flour
8tbsp sugar substitute
30g (1oz) chopped almonds
 or pecans
60g (2 ½oz) soft margarine,
 non-hydrogenated
1tsp grated orange zest
½tsp ground cinnamon
¼tsp ground cardamom

1 Preheat the oven to 180°C, Gas 4. In a bowl, toss the plums with the sugar substitute, cornflour, ginger and cinnamon. Arrange evenly in a 23cm (9-inch) deep pie plate.
2 For the topping: Combine the oats, flour, sugar substitute, almonds, margarine, orange zest, cinnamon and cardamom in a bowl. Using your fingers, rub the ingredients together until the mixture forms a crumbly dough.
3 Sprinkle evenly over the fruit mixture. Bake for 35–40 minutes or until the topping is golden and the fruit mixture is bubbling.

Serves 6

BASICS

BASIC TOMATO SAUCE

You can chill this sauce or freeze it in batches to have on hand to use in other recipes.

Makes about 1.5 litres (2³/4 pints), enough for 3–4 batches

  1tbsp olive oil

  2 onions, chopped

  3 cloves of garlic, minced

  1 large carrot, finely grated

  4x400g cans chopped tomatoes

  2tbsp tomato purée

  2tsp dried basil

  1tsp dried oregano

  ½tsp each sea salt and freshly ground black pepper

1 In a large saucepan or deep frying pan, heat the oil over a medium heat. Cook the onions, garlic and carrot, stirring often, for 8 minutes or until softened.

2 Add the tomatoes, tomato puréée, basil, oregano and seasoning, then bring to the boil. Reduce the heat to medium and simmer, uncovered, for 30 minutes or until thickened slightly.

Storage: This will keep refrigerated for up to a week, or will freeze for up to 2 months.

VARIATIONS FOR EACH BATCH OF SAUCE:

Three-Mushroom Tomato Sauce:
In a bowl, pour in enough boiling water to cover 25g (1oz) dried porcini (cep) mushrooms, and soak for 15 minutes. Meanwhile, in a frying pan, heat 2tsp olive oil over a medium heat; cook 125g (4oz) each of chopped button mushrooms and chopped fresh shiitake mushrooms for 5 minutes or until golden. Drain the porcini and stir into the mushroom mixture. Stir in a batch of Basic Tomato Sauce and simmer for 10 minutes. Toss with 300g (10oz) cooked pasta.
Makes 4 servings.

Tricolore Vegetable Tomato Sauce:
In a frying pan, heat 2tsp olive oil over a medium heat. Cook half a yellow and half a red pepper, chopped, half a courgette, chopped, and 125g (4oz) cut green beans for 6–8 minutes or until the vegetables are softened. Add a batch of Basic Tomato Sauce and simmer for 10 minutes. Toss with 300g (10oz) cooked pasta. Makes 4 servings.

Puttanesca Sauce:
In a deep frying pan over a medium heat, bring to the boil a batch of Basic Tomato Sauce, 3 anchovy fillets, chopped, ¹/4tsp hot chilli-pepper flakes, 75g (3oz) pitted black olives, halved, and 2tbsp capers, drained. Reduce the heat and simmer for 20 minutes or until thick. Toss with 300g (10oz) cooked spaghetti. Sprinkle the servings with chopped fresh basil, parsley and a little grated Parmesan cheese.
Makes 4 servings.

Rocket and Roasted Garlic Tomato:
Sauce: In a deep frying pan over a medium heat, bring to the boil a batch of Basic Tomato Sauce. Reduce the heat and stir in the garlic squeezed from 1 head of roasted garlic (follow the instructions for roasting garlic in Mushroom Soup recipe, page 43) and 1x100g bag of rocket. Simmer, stirring, until the rocket is wilted, about 2 minutes. Toss with 300g (10oz) cooked pasta. Sprinkle the servings with a little grated Parmesan cheese or crumbled goats' cheese.
Makes 4 servings.

Gi PESTO

The addition of water along with the oil in this pesto reduces the fat content. It gives the pesto a lighter green colour than traditional pesto, but it tastes great.

 125g (4oz) fresh basil leaves
 3 cloves of garlic
 50g (2oz) sunflower seeds
 15g (½oz) grated fresh Parmesan cheese
 1½tbsp lemon juice
 ¼tsp each sea salt and freshly ground black
   pepper
 3tbsp extra-virgin olive oil

1 In a food processor, purée the basil, garlic, sunflower seeds, Parmesan, lemon juice and salt and pepper. With the motor running, add 3tbsp water and oil in a steady stream.

Storage: Store in an airtight container and chill for up to 3 days or freeze for up to 6 months.

Tip: When basil is plentiful, make a double batch and freeze in ice- cube trays. When frozen, remove from the tray and store in an airtight container in the freezer. Then you'll always have a bit of pesto on hand to stir into hot pasta or soups.
Makes 200g (7 oz)

CRANBERRY AND ORANGE SAUCE

This is great served with the Turkey-Quinoa Loaf (see recipe on page 74) or a simple roast turkey breast.

 250g (9oz) fresh or frozen cranberries
 50g (2oz) dried cranberries
 3tbsp sugar substitute
 4tbsp fresh orange juice
 2tbsp Grand Marnier or any orange-flavoured liqueur
   (optional)
 1tbsp frozen orange juice concentrate
 1tbsp grated orange zest
 ½tsp cinnamon

1 In a saucepan, combine the cranberries, dried cranberries, sugar substitute, orange juice, Grand Marnier (if using), orange juice concentrate, orange zest and cinnamon; bring to the boil. Reduce the heat to a simmer and cook, stirring occasionally, for 10 minutes or until the cranberries burst and the sauce is thickened.
Makes about 300g (10oz)

STRAINED YOGHURT

Place some natural low-fat yogurt in a sieve lined with cheesecloth or a coffee filter. Place the sieve over a bowl. Cover with clingfilm and chill for at least 1 hour or up to 4 hours. Discard the liquid that drains off and transfer the yogurt to another bowl. Sweeten to taste if liked.

GARAM MASALA

There are myriad recipes for this Indian spice blend. Every family in northern India has its own version. You can buy it pre-packaged, but a homemade mixture is infinitely better tasting.

 3 cinnamon sticks, broken
 2 dried bay leaves
 1 tbsp green Cardamom pods
 1 tbsp coriander seeds
 2 tsp black peppercorns
 2 tsp cumin seeds
 2 tsp whole cloves
 2 tsp fennel seeds
 ½tsp ground nutmeg

1 Place all ingredients on a baking sheet and roast in 150°C, Gas 2 oven for 10 minutes or until fragrant. Transfer to a spice grinder or clean coffee grinder and grind finely. Store in an airtight container for up to 6 months.

SEASONAL MENUS

SPRINGTIME TEA IN THE GARDEN
Lemony Lentil and Rice Soup
Salmon, Red Potato and Asparagus Salad
Fruit Salad
Strawberry Tea Bread

MID-SUMMER'S EVE BARBECUE
Mediterranean Summer Salad
Red Bean Tabbouleh
Spicy Roasted Chicken with Tomatoes and Tarragon
Blueberry Beef Burgers
Lemon Crème Fraiche Ice Cream with Fresh Berries

AUTUMN HARVEST BISTRO DINNER
Mixed Greens with Roasted Pears,
   Pecans and Chevre
Blanquette de Veau
Apple Upside-Down Cake

FESTIVE SEASON BUFFET
Red Lentil Hummus with Basmati Rice Crackers
Spinach Bites
Fruit and Nut Stuffed Turkey Breast
Vegetable Cassoulet
Celeriac Slaw
Cranberry-Almond Biscotti with Decaffeinated Coffee

INDEX